FREEZE FRAME

A PHOTOGRAPHIC HISTORY OF
THE WINTER OLYMPICS

As the sun sets on the final day of competition at the 1998 Winter Games, the Olympic flame burns brightly over Nagano, Japan.

FREEZE
FRAME

A PHOTOGRAPHIC HISTORY OF
THE WINTER OLYMPICS

BY SUE MACY • FOREWORD BY PEGGY FLEMING

NATIONAL GEOGRAPHIC

WASHINGTON, D.C.

For my uncle and aunt, Bill and Freda Macy, with love

ACKNOWLEDGMENTS

I'd like to express my appreciation to Michael Salmon and his colleagues at the library of the Amateur Athletic Foundation of Los Angeles for their gracious help and hospitality. Thanks also to all the folks who aided me in gathering the photographs in this book, including Mike LeTourneau of the Associated Press, Laura Hitchcock of Empics, and the staffs of Getty Images, Corbis, and the photo archives of the Olympic Museum in Lausanne, Switzerland. I also owe much to the photographers whose work is represented here. Their "freeze frames" of Olympic action captured the excitement of the Games and kept it alive for generations to come.

Every book is a collaborative effort, but those that are highly visual depend even more on the combined contributions of a number of people. I thank my brilliant designer, Marty Ittner, my equally brilliant and superbly supportive editor, Jennifer Emmett, and the other terrific folks at National Geographic, led by the ever wise and wonderful Nancy Feresten, for making this book a reality.

On a personal note I thank my brother, Buddy Macy, my parents, Ruth and Morris Macy, and my partner, Sheila Wolinsky, for their continued love, patience, and support. I also thank Sue Rodin and Ernestine Miller for their encouragement and generosity in sharing their innumerable contacts in the sports world. This book is dedicated to my aunt, Freda Macy, and my uncle, Bill Macy, now 90 years old, who regrets that his own winter sports career was cut short when he rode his childhood sled into a mailbox.

FRONT COVER: Canada's Clara Hughes is the picture of joy and determination as she powers her way to the bronze medal in the women's 5,000-meter speed skating event at the 2002 Winter Games. Hughes, who also won two bronze medals in cycling at the Summer Games in Atlanta, is one of only four athletes to medal at both the Winter and Summer Olympics.

BACK COVER: Austrian skier Hermann Maier (top) attacks the giant slalom course on the way to his second gold medal at the 1998 Nagano Games, and 11-year-old Sonja Henie of Norway competes in her first Olympics in 1924. Though she finished last, Henie would go on to win gold medals in figure skating in 1928, 1932, and 1936. BACKGROUND: Therry Brunner of Switzerland catches air during the men's halfpipe snowboarding event at the 2002 Winter Games.

Book design is by Marty Ittner.
The body text of the book is set in Scala.
The display text is set in Base 9 SC.

Published with permission from the United States Olympic Committee and the International Olympic Committee. (Authenticating statement 36USC220506)

Library of Congress Cataloging-in-Publication Data
Macy, Sue.
Freeze Frame : a photographic history of the Winter Olympics
by Sue Macy; foreword by Peggy Fleming.
        p. cm.
Includes bibliographical references and index.
1. Winter Olympics—History—Juvenile literature.
2. Winter Olympics—History—Pictorial works—juvenile literature.
I. Title.
GV841.5.M33 2006
796.98—dc22
                                        2005012948

Hardcover ISBN: 0-7922-7887-9
Library Edition ISBN 0-7922-7888-7

Printed in the United States of America

CONTENTS

Olympic Torch,
1964 Winter
Games

I N MY SPORT OF FIGURE SKATING, an Olympic gold medal is the ultimate title. National championships and world championships don't get quite the same attention as the Olympics. There's not the magnitude associated with those titles that there is with the Olympic title. Olympic figure skating has a long history going all the way back to 1908, when skaters competed for medals as part of the Summer Games. That's why it's an awesome feeling to be an Olympic champion.

I went to my first Olympics when I was 15 years old and it was a total surprise. I had never dreamed that I would have a chance to go. I was competing in the seniors for the first time at the 1964 U.S. national championships and ended up winning. That was a big enough shock, but that year, the Nationals were also the Olympic Trials for the games in Innsbruck, Austria. I had never been to Europe before and had never even skated outdoors. Growing up in California, all of our skating rinks were indoors. At Innsbruck, we practiced outside and had our competition inside. At those Games, I did everything from marching in the opening parade to meeting athletes from other countries in the Olympic Village. All of it was so overwhelming, in a good way. I ended up finishing sixth out of 30 skaters, even with the flu. Sjoukje Dijkstra of the Netherlands, who'd won the silver medal in 1960, took the gold.

By the time I went to Grenoble, France, for the 1968 Winter Games, I had won the U.S. national title five years in a row and the world championship title twice. It was a completely different scenario from 1964. I was the favorite and had to deal with that pressure. I really didn't want to let anyone down. I didn't march in the parade or stay in the village the whole time. I was there to get a job done.

Winning that Olympic gold medal completely changed my life. The 1968 Winter Games were the first to be broadcast live and in color via satellite around the world. I was the only U.S. gold medalist at those Games, and it became a big story because the Olympics and skating were suddenly reaching a mass audience.

Fortunately, I was able to use the discipline and poise that I had developed

FOREWORD

BY PEGGY FLEMING

on the ice in this new stage of my life. Skating was a wonderful tool for me to find out what I was made of, how strong I was, and where my weak points were. It gave me confidence. It helped me know myself and tested my nerve. All of that came in handy as I embarked on an uncharted skating career with the glare of the spotlight shining on me.

I think the healthiest way to consider going into a sport is to really love it, and just love getting better. If you go into it thinking, "Oh, I have to win, I won't be satisfied unless I win," I don't think it will serve you well. I don't think you'll learn as much. And it's all about learning. Participating in sports should better you, even at the highest level. The Olympics is just a stepping-stone to the rest of your life.

I MIGHT AS WELL ADMIT IT at the very start of this book. I hate the cold. It makes my nose run, my lips crack, my hands turn into chapped monster claws. When the thermometer dips below freezing, I wrap myself in flannel and wool and stay as close to the radiator as humanly possible. Which makes it even more astounding that on March 10, 2002, I voluntarily stood outside for five hours in below-zero-with-the-wind-chill temperatures to wait for an Olympic champion.

It wasn't just any champion. Sixteen-year-old Sarah Hughes provided the feel-good story of the 2002 Winter Games, storming from fourth place to first with a flawless figure skating routine that was filled with youthful exuberance and seven triple jumps. Her astonishment at learning that she'd won the gold was a refreshing surprise in a sports world increasingly dominated by commercialism and controversy. Added to that, she was a local hero. Hughes lived less than an hour from me and trained at a rink just 10 minutes from my New Jersey home. I wanted to be part of the crowd when her neighbors cheered her accomplishments with a homecoming parade.

By the time Hughes and her entourage appeared, my face was frozen and my extremities were numb. But as I stood listening to everyone from her classmates to the local deli owner sing her praises, I reflected on the impact that Hughes had on her community. People in her hometown took pride in her victory, and with the horrors of the terrorist attacks of September 11, 2001, fresh in our minds, we all seemed reassured that someone who worked hard and played by the rules could still come out on top. Hughes's drive and passion inspired us to believe in the possibilities for success in our own lives. We were elevated by her example and thrilled to share in it, if only as frozen faces in a crowd of admirers.

On a larger scale, the safe, successful realization of the 2002 Winter Games was a welcome development in a world still stunned by the violence of September 11. This gathering of athletes from 77 nations spanned political ideologies to promote peace and human dignity through sport. As they competed in the spirit of friendship and fair play, the athletes gave us hope that the wounds inflicted the previous

INTRODUCTION

September might one day heal. In an atmosphere that was sometimes solemn but often joyous, the Games in Salt Lake City helped the United States and the world take the first steps back to normality.

It seems appropriate that those steps were taken on ground covered with freshly fallen snow. The untainted landscapes of Winter Olympic venues make it easy to think of new beginnings. And the enthusiasm of the athletes makes it hard not to get caught up in the drama, even if you don't ski or skate yourself and even if you hate the cold. The Olympic Winter Games are more intimate than their summer equivalents, with roughly one-quarter the number of athletes, sports, and events. But throughout their history, they have produced their own brand of heroes and villains, triumphs and scandals. This book will look at some of the touching, awe-inspiring, surprising, and occasionally bizarre events have shaped the Winter Games and introduce you to some of the athletes whose achievements are frozen in time.

All three medals in the women's downhill went to Austrians in 1964, with ★ CHRISTL HAAS ★ taking the gold. Haas would return to the Winter Games in 1968 to win the bronze in the same event.

★ DEBI THOMAS ★ of the U.S. becomes the first black athlete to win a medal at the Winter Games when she takes the bronze in figure skating in 1988.

In 2002, the ★ NETHERLANDS 1 ★ bobsled team competes in one of its heats. The team did not finish in medal contention.

★ MAMI SHINDO ★ of Japan, left, and ★ OLENA PETROVA ★ of the Ukraine carry their guns on their backs as they race in the women's 15-kilometer biathlon in 2002.

★ LEA ANN PARSLEY ★ of the U.S. has her eyes on the prize as she takes a skeleton training run in Salt Lake City. Parsley would win the silver medal.

Austrians ★ ELISABETH "SISSY" SCHWARTZ ★ and ★ KURT OPPELT ★ skate their way to the pairs gold medal in 1956. Foreshadowing future scandals, crowds at this competition objected so strongly to the scores of some skaters that they threw oranges at the judges.

★ PAAL TRULSEN ★ delivers the stone for the Norwegian team in the gold medal curling match at the 2002 Winter Games. Norway beat Canada to take the gold.

SLIDING

Antique ice skate and boot

★ DEREK PARRA ★ of the U.S. sets a world record and wins the gold medal in the men's 1,500-meter speed skating race in 2002. Ten days earlier, Parra won the silver medal in the 5,000 meters.

★ RIKKA NIEMINEN ★ of Finland slides into U.S. goalie ★ SARA DECOSTA ★ in the early rounds of women's hockey in 2002. The U.S. would go on to win the silver medal.

Charles Jewtraw, 23, learned to skate at the local speed skating rink in Lake Placid, New York, where his father was caretaker. He would donate his 1924 gold medal, the first ever awarded at the Olympic Winter Games, to the Smithsonian Institution in Washington, D.C. Top, an antique skate from the collection of the Olympic Museum in Lausanne, Switzerland.

ON A CRISP, CLEAR JANUARY AFTERNOON in 1924, close to 300 athletes took part in a curious parade through the snow-covered streets of Chamonix, France. To the polite applause of the spectators lining the way, they marched carrying their skis, poles, skates, and hockey sticks and dragging their bobsleds behind them. The athletes, including about a dozen women, had journeyed from the United States,

THIS SNOWY
PRELUDE

Canada, and 14 European nations to take part in the first winter sports competition ever authorized by the International Olympic Committee (IOC). Over the next 11 days, these skiers, skaters, bobsledders, and hockey players would make history.

Amid the pageantry, some of the skaters in the U.S. delegation were just happy to be on solid ground. Their ten-day voyage on the *President Monroe* ocean liner was unusually rough, and speed skater Joe Moore of New York City had been seasick the entire time. At least Charles Jewtraw of Lake Placid, New York, said he felt like his old self after reaching land and getting a good night's sleep. Both Jewtraw and Moore were set to take part in the first event, the 500-meter speed skating race.

POSTER ADVERTISING THE
MONTENVERS RAILWAY THAT
CONNECTS CHAMONIX TO THE MER
DE GLACE GLACIER, CIRCA 1910

BARON PIERRE DE COUBERTIN,
FOUNDER OF THE MODERN OLYMPIC
GAMES, HAD MIXED FEELINGS ABOUT
THE INCLUSION OF WINTER SPORTS.

Officially, Jewtraw, Moore, and the other athletes had come to France to take part in an International Winter Sports Week. The IOC didn't rename the gathering the First Olympic Winter Games until two years later, after it decided to make winter competitions a regular part of the Olympic schedule. The tentative nature of the Chamonix sports festival reflected years of debate among IOC members as to the place of winter sports at the Olympics. The modern Olympic Games were inspired by competitions held in ancient Greece that included running, boxing, wrestling, and other sports generally contested in warm weather. When Frenchman Pierre de Coubertin called a meeting in 1894 to plan the first modern Olympics, delegates concentrated on these "summer sports." The only cold-weather discipline on the roster for the 1896 Olympics was figure skating, but since the host city of Athens, Greece, didn't have an ice rink, no events took place.

There were other factors behind the IOC's lack of enthusiasm for winter sports. Timing was a major problem. Since skiing and ski jumping were outdoor events that required cold weather, they could not be contested in summer. Beyond that, at the turn of the century, few countries had the facilities for competitions in these sports, and few outside of Scandinavia had world-class winter athletes to represent them. As Coubertin wrote in 1901, "England, Germany, Holland, and Russia, as well as southern regions, will have great difficulty furnishing capable champions to fight vigorously against Sweden, Norway, and Finland." Ice hockey and skating were more widespread, since the invention of artificial ice made it possible to maintain indoor ice rinks year-round. But as was evidenced in 1896, there was no guarantee that a city chosen to host the Olympic Games would have a rink.

Surprisingly, the greatest opposition to the idea of winter sports at the Olympics came from the Scandinavians. In 1901, Viktor Balck of Sweden organized the Nordic Games, an international winter sports competition and cultural festival held roughly every four years in Sweden or Norway. Called "the father of Swedish sport," Balck was one of the original members of the IOC and a great friend of Coubertin. His idea was to encourage national pride and tourism by holding a winter event that was similar to, but separate from, the Olympics. "Above all we placed the national goal of rendering a service to the fatherland and bringing honor to our country," Balck explained in 1909. "The Nordic Games have now become a national concern for our entire people."

Very quickly, the Nordic Games became such a source of Scandinavian pride that Balck fought all attempts to make them part of the Olympic movement or even to add winter sports to the Olympic program. Despite his efforts, figure skating was finally contested at the Summer Olympics in 1908. Fourteen men and seven women from six nations competed for medals at Princes Skating Club in Knightsbridge, London. The women's individual title went to Florence "Madge" Syers of Great Britain, who had made news six years earlier when she came in second at the otherwise all-male world skating championships. Here, Syers also teamed with her husband, Edgar, to take the bronze medal in the pairs event. Anna Hübler and Heinrich Burger of Germany won the gold medal in pairs skating, while Sweden's Ulrich Salchow won the men's individual gold. Salchow, who complimented the IOC on the "splendid arrangements" for the skating competition, is remembered today for the backward salchow jump that he invented in 1907.

ULRICH SALCHOW, ABOVE,

INVENTED THE FAMOUS SALCHOW

JUMP IN WHICH A SKATER

TAKES OFF FROM THE BACK

INNER EDGE OF ONE FOOT AND

LANDS ON THE BACK OUTER

EDGE OF THE OPPOSITE FOOT.

Although some IOC members suggested adding more winter sports to the 1912 Summer Olympics, slated to take place on Viktor Balck's home turf of Stockholm, Sweden, Balck rejected the idea. In fact, even figure skating was dropped from the program. Plans for the 1916 Summer Olympics included skating, ice hockey, cross country skiing, and ski jumping, but due to World War I, those Games never took place. When the Summer Olympics resumed in Antwerp, Belgium, in 1920, figure skating was back on the program and ice hockey was added for the first time. Scandinavians dominated the figure skating events, but in ice hockey, teams from European countries were no match for the United States or Canada. In a memorable game against Switzerland, the U.S. netted a goal during each of the first 13 minutes and won by a score of 29–0. Canada's team of "ragtag immigrant kids" from Winnipeg, Manitoba, scored fewer goals than the U.S. overall, but shut out their North American neighbors 2–0 to win the gold medal. The U.S. took the silver.

Viktor Balck left the IOC in 1921, and that year the group returned to the debate on whether to add more winter sports to the Olympic program. The French, Swiss, and Canadians were strongly behind the idea, but the Scandinavian nations still opposed it. Finally, the delegates reached a compromise. The IOC decided to hold an International Winter Sports Week several months before the 1924 Summer Olympics. "This snowy prelude" to the Olympics, as Pierre de Coubertin called it, would help the IOC gauge the amount of interest and the level of competition in winter sports. Since the Summer Olympics would be in Paris, the IOC chose another French town, Chamonix, for the Winter Sports Week. To get ready, this town of 3,000 people built a figure skating rink, a hockey rink, and a ski jumping hill.

Canada's ice hockey team, above, defeated the U.S. 6-1 to win the gold medal on February 3, 1924, in outdoor action shown below. As the final ended, officials announced that former U.S. president Woodrow Wilson had died earlier that day.

During the 11 days of competition, athletes took part in figure skating, speed skating, ice hockey, Nordic skiing, bobsled, and the demonstration sports of curling and an event similar to biathlon. Figure skating consisted of the men's and women's individual contests and the pairs. Speed skating featured races of 500 meters, 1,500 meters, 5,000 meters, and 10,000 meters. Nordic skiing included cross country skiing races of 18 kilometers and 50 kilometers, as well as ski jumping on a 90-meter hill and a combined event with two ski jumps and a cross country race. There was one four-man bobsled contest. In the biathlon-like demonstration event, athletes with rifles skied cross country, stopping at specific points to rest their rifles on crossed ski poles and shoot at targets. All events other than figure skating were open only to men.

Scandinavian athletes ended up winning 28 of the 43 medals awarded, with 17 of them going to Norwegians. But Charles Jewtraw did the folks in Lake Placid proud when he won a gold medal in the 500-meter speed skating race. It would be the only gold awarded to an athlete from the U.S. (still reeling from his rough sea voyage, Joe Moore came in eighth). Finland's A. Clas Thunberg won both the 1,500- and 5,000-meter speed skating races and was ahead in the 10,000 until he pulled back and Julius Skutnabb beat him. One magazine wrote that Thunberg finished second, "only it seemed out of courtesy to his teammate Skutnabb." Indeed, Thunberg later revealed that before the race, Skutnabb had asked Thunberg to let him win. "I was really pleased to make this gesture," Thunberg said. Even with this sacrifice, he came away from Chamonix with a good haul: two gold medals, one silver, and one bronze.

Norwegian jumpers swept the medals in ski jumping, or so the record books reported for 50 years. Jacob

Tullin Thams won the gold. Narve Bonna took the silver. And Nordic athlete extraordinaire Thorleif Haug was awarded the bronze. Haug also earned three gold medals at Chamonix, winning both of the cross country races and the Nordic combined. However, when the Norwegian athletes from these Olympics got together in 1974 to celebrate the 50th anniversary of the Winter Games, a sports historian checked the math on the ski jumping scores and found a mistake. Haug actually had come in fourth, behind Anders Haugen of the U.S. Haug had gone to his grave thinking he'd won the bronze medal, but Haugen finally received his prize at age 85. It was presented to him by Haug's daughter and remains the only Olympic ski jumping medal ever won by a U.S. athlete.

As predicted, the ice hockey battle came down to the squads from the U.S. and Canada, with the Canadians showing excellent teamwork and the U.S. powered by brilliant individual efforts. U.S. goalkeeper Alphonse La Croix did not give up a single goal until the gold medal game, but the first one seemed to open the floodgates. Canada scored six times, while the U.S. scored only once, giving Canada the gold medal and the U.S. the silver. Meanwhile, in figure skating, Beatrix Loughran, called "a cheerful American girl" by the U.S. press, fought the "stately, somber Austrian woman," Herma Planck-Szabó. The Austrian won, though one judge admitted that she might have received some votes because she was older and Loughran would have many more chances to win in the future. Planck-Szabó herself had little patience with young skaters. "I do not like to compete against children," she said, specifically referring to 11-year-old entrant Sonja Henie of Norway. Though Henie finished dead last, she would eventually become the most successful Olympic figure skater of all time.

In the end, the sports week at Chamonix was deemed a "great success" by none other than Pierre de Coubertin. Never a staunch supporter of winter sports at the Olympics, Coubertin seemed to have mellowed on the subject by the time he spoke at the closing ceremonies. "Winter sports are among the purest," he said, "and that is why I was so eager to see them take their place in a definitive way among the Olympic events." He was not alone. At a 1925 meeting, the IOC decided to continue holding separate Olympic Winter Games during the same calendar years as the Summer Olympics. Soon afterward, the group voted to rename the Chamonix sports week the "First Olympic Winter Games." With Coubertin retiring in 1925, the Olympic Movement entered a new era, one in which winter sports would be on equal footing with the summer events that started it all.

ON THE FIRST DAY OF THE 1968 WINTER OLYMPICS IN GRENOBLE, FRANCE, AN UNIDENTIFIED
SPEED SKATER CARRIES AN UMBRELLA AS SHE PRACTICES IN THE FALLING SNOW. TOP, A POSTCARD
FROM A VISITOR TO LAKE PLACID SIX DAYS BEFORE THE START OF THE 1932 WINTER GAMES WARNS,
"NOW IT IS RAIN AND SNOW. IF WEATHER DOES NOT CHANGE THERE WILL BE NO OLYMPICS."

CHAPTER 2

SPORTSWRITER ARTHUR DALEY, who covered the Olympics for the *New York Times* for 40 years, often wrote that there was one thing the organizers of any Winter Games could count on: The weather would drive them crazy. Temperatures would rise instead of falling. Ice would melt instead of freezing. It would snow too much, or not at all. Winds would kick up, fog would descend, or

THE INESCAPABLE WEATHER JINX

lightning would streak across the sky. Daley called it the "weather jinx," and he told his readers that it was as much a part of the Winter Games as ski boots and heavy sweaters. "The weather gods seem to delight in playing the vilest pranks on all Olympic Winter Games," Daley wrote in 1964. "There is no escape from the weather jinx."

Indeed, the organizers of almost every edition of the Winter Olympics have had to contend with some sort of weather emergency. The problems began in 1924 when a storm dumped three feet of snow on the outdoor speed skating rink at Chamonix a week before the start of the Games. As officials were making plans to haul away the snow, the town was socked with drenching rains that threatened

WITH ARTISTIC CHOREOGRAPHY, A TEAM OF MEN CLEARS THE SNOW FROM AN OUTDOOR ICE RINK AT THE 1936 WINTER GAMES IN GARMISCH-PARTENKIRCHEN, GERMANY. THE GAMES HAD OPENED IN A BLINDING SNOWSTORM, THOUGH EXTRA SNOW STILL WAS NEEDED TO SHORE UP THE SKI JUMP AND LANDING HILL.

to turn the rink into a lake. Fortunately a sudden freeze right before the opening ceremonies allowed the Games to go on without delay. But Pierre de Coubertin recognized the impact of weather when he recounted the events at Chamonix in his *Olympic Memoirs*. "The thaw," he wrote, "will always be the great drawback of these Winter Games."

At the 1928 Winter Olympics in St. Moritz, Switzerland, the weather jinx was working overtime, resulting in the most sudden and bizarre weather changes in the history of the Games. On February 14, after a night of light snow showers, the athletes in the 50-kilometer cross-country race set out at 8 a.m. with the temperature at 0° Fahrenheit. During the race, St. Moritz experienced a *föhn*, a strong dry wind that carries warm weather down a mountain. By midday the temperature had soared to 77° Fahrenheit, and the skiers had no choice but to slog through the melting snow. The winner of the race, Per Erik Hedlund of Sweden, finished in just over 4 hours, 52 minutes. That was more than an hour slower than the winning time in the same race at the 1924 Winter Games. Meanwhile, the summerlike conditions forced officials to suspend competition in the 10,000-meter speed skating race before all of the skaters had finished their heats. By the time it was cold enough to resume racing several days later, many competitors had gone home. Some record books show the winner of the 10,000 to be Irving Jaffee of the U.S., who had clocked the fastest time before the thaw, but in fact no medals were awarded because the race was never finished.

After St. Moritz, organizers of the Winter Games did their best to build extra days into the schedule to counteract the chaos caused by Mother Nature. They also took other creative steps as necessary. For example, even though the 1936 Games in the German towns of Garmisch and Partenkirchen opened in a blinding snowstorm, officials found that they needed more snow on the ski jump and its landing hill. They corrected the situation by bringing truckloads of snow to those areas. Similarly, when another föhn threatened the 1964 Winter Games at Innsbruck, Austria, the Austrian army carried ice and snow down from various mountaintops to reinforce the bobsled and luge runs and the Alpine skiing courses.

Two months before the 1960 Winter Games at Squaw Valley, California, officials took a spiritual approach by inviting Native Americans from a nearby Paiute tribe to do a ceremonial dance aimed at ensuring cold weather. The temperature immediately went up five degrees, and as the opening ceremonies drew nearer, torrential rains accompanied by 100-mile-per-hour winds raged all around. Fortunately, temperatures finally fell and the rain evolved into a 24-hour blizzard that turned the area into a winter wonderland.

As time passed, scientific innovations helped organizers of the Winter Games overcome at least some of the problems that Mother Nature threw their way. Beginning in 1980 at Lake Placid, artificial snow was used to shore up the Alpine and Nordic skiing courses.

WATCHING THE ACTION AT THE 1960 WINTER GAMES WAS ITSELF AN EXTREME SPORT, AS IS EVIDENCED BY THIS SNOW-COVERED SPECTATOR.

SPECTATORS REACT TO THE POSTPONEMENT OF THE ALPINE SKIING EVENTS AT THE 1998 WINTER GAMES. AFTER THE TORCH WAS EXTINGUISHED, *CNN/SPORTS ILLUSTRATED* POSTULATED THAT THE NAGANO OLYMPIAD "MAY BEST BE REMEMBERED FOR ITS WEATHER PROBLEMS AND THE GRACIOUSNESS OF ITS HOSTS."

IN 1960, OLYMPIC OFFICIALS
CALLED OUT THE U.S. MARINES
TO PACK DOWN THE SNOW ON THE
SKI RUNS AT SQUAW VALLEY.

And although it was less expensive to hold skating contests outdoors on frozen lakes or ponds, figure skating events finally were moved to indoor arenas with artificial ice in 1960. The speed skating contests followed in 1988. While bobsled, luge, and skeleton competitions still take place outdoors, the tracks are now covered with artificial ice.

For those athletes who compete outside, particularly in the Nordic and Alpine skiing events, the weather is always an issue. Windy conditions can interfere with ski jumping events or even cause them to be postponed. The rules of biathlon state that races cannot be run if the air temperature is colder than −4° Fahrenheit (−20° Celsius). Skiers need to use different types of wax, and even different skis, depending on how soft or icy the course is. At the 1998 Winter Games, Norwegian cross country skier Bjørn Dæhlie chose the wrong wax for the freshly fallen snow in the 30-kilometer race and ended up finishing 20th, though he had been favored to win. "Your arena is constantly changing—the light, the visibility," said Donna Weinbrecht, the 1992 gold medalist in women's mogul skiing. "From minute to minute the course can change. And you have to accept....what has been given to you."

Despite all of the innovations and the moving of most ice events indoors, the weather continues to be the X factor in any Winter Games. High winds of up to 20 miles per hour postponed the women's downhill at Salt Lake City in 2002, and snow, freezing rain, and heavy fog combined to throw the schedule at the 1998 Games in Nagano, Japan, into complete disarray. Five of the first eight days of Alpine skiing in 1998 were complete washouts, and not a single Alpine event went off as scheduled during that time. Bobsled, biathlon, snowboarding, and ski jumping events also were postponed or delayed. Said Picabo Street, the

CARRYING THEIR RIFLES ON THEIR BACKS, ATHLETES FROM 19 NATIONS BRAVED THE HEAVIEST SNOWFALL OF THE 2002 WINTER GAMES TO COMPETE IN THE MEN'S 4 X 7.5-KILOMETER BIATHLON RELAY. THE TEAM FROM NORWAY TOOK THE GOLD, WHILE GERMANY WON THE SILVER AND FRANCE WON THE BRONZE.

favorite and eventual gold medalist in the women's super G, "You want snow because it's a winter event, but it's like 'We've got enough now, thank you.'" Yet the bad weather turned out to be the saving grace for one skier at Nagano. Austria's Hermann Maier took a horrific fall during the men's downhill, flying some 30 yards in the air before landing on his head, somersaulting through two safety nets, and coming to a stop in a pile of snow. Maier was scheduled to compete in the men's super G the next day, but two postponements gave him extra time to rest and recover. He came back three days after his crash to win the gold medal in the super G and went on to take the gold in the giant slalom as well.

Ultimately, athletes and organizers alike seem to accept weather problems as just one of the challenges to be met on the way to a successful Olympic Winter Games. As for spectators, Arthur Daley once noted that they have another option. The Winter Olympics "will be piped into warm living rooms by television," Daley pointed out in the *New York Times* in 1960. "No one will have to subject himself to frostbite, piercing cold, discomfort and other miseries. If you must have winter sports, that is the way to take them."

After winning two silver medals in 1956 and two bronze medals in 1964, Italy's Eugenio Monti led his country's two- and four-man bobsled teams to gold medals in 1968. A downhill skier whose promising career was cut short by injury, the "Flying Redhead" was 40 years old when he finally won the gold. Here, Monti steers the bobsled in the final heat of the four-man race in 1968. Top, an early bobsled, circa 1910.

EUGENIO MONTI OF ITALY won two gold medals in bobsledding at the 1968 Winter Games, but he is remembered best for a race in which he finished third. At Innsbruck in 1964, Monti and his brakeman, Sergio Siorpaes, had already completed both of their runs in the two-man bobsled when they heard that their opponents from Great Britain had a problem. Tony Nash and Robin Dixon had broken

HEROES AND
SUPERSTARS

a bolt that held the runners of their sled to the shell, making it impossible for them to take their second run. Monti quickly removed the bolt from his own sled and had someone rush it up to Nash and Dixon at the top of the course. They substituted Monti's bolt for the broken one and then raced down the track with such speed that they won the gold medal, bumping Monti and Siorpaes from second place to third. "As far as I was concerned," Monti later said, "Tony and Robin would have done the same for me." But Olympic officials were so impressed with Monti's selfless act that they awarded him the first ever Pierre de Coubertin International Trophy for Fair Play.

SONJA HENIE DANCES WITH ACTOR
CESAR ROMERO IN THE MOTION
PICTURE *WINTERTIME* IN 1943.
JUST A FEW YEARS EARLIER,
IN 1938, HENIE WAS THE THIRD
BIGGEST BOX OFFICE DRAW IN
HOLLYWOOD BEHIND CHILD STAR
SHIRLEY TEMPLE AND HEARTTHROB
CLARK GABLE.

At their best, the Olympic Winter Games showcase the noble sacrifices and brilliant triumphs of the top athletes in winter sports. These heroes and superstars compete against themselves, their opponents, and Mother Nature to achieve performances of great beauty, courage, and daring. Some are remembered for the medals they've won, others for their acts of kindness or the hardships they've overcome. Their efforts set the standard for all of the athletes who represent their nations at the Olympics.

Sonja Henie was only 11 years old when she skated at Chamonix in 1924, but she quickly became one of the world's most renowned athletes. Already a national champion in Norway, she revolutionized figure skating by using ballet-like moves to link the required technical elements of her program. Henie finished last at the 1924 Games, partly because she kept skating over to the sidelines to ask her coach what to do next. But she went on to win gold medals in 1928, 1932, and 1936. After that Henie turned professional, performing in ice shows and starring in 11 motion pictures. Her films, with titles including *Thin Ice* and *Wintertime*, made Henie a millionaire and helped popularize figure skating around the world. She died of leukemia in 1969 at age 57.

Billy Fiske also competed in his first Winter Games at a young age, and in fact for over 60 years he held the record as the youngest man to win a gold medal. Fiske was just 16 when he convinced the chairman of the U.S. Olympic Bobsled Committee to enter a second sled in the 1928 Winter Olympics with him as the driver. Although most of his teammates had never even seen a bobsled before their first practice, Fiske drove them to the gold. Four years later, he won again with a crew that included Jay O'Brien, the oldest man ever to win a gold medal at the Winter Games. Fiske

BECAUSE THE U.S. FOUR-MAN BOBSLED TEAM TOOK HOME THE GOLD MEDAL AT THE 1932 WINTER GAMES, THEY ALSO WON THE MARTINEAU CHALLENGE CUP, GIVEN TO THE WORLD'S TOP BOBSLED SQUAD. HERE, BILLY FISKE ACCEPTS THE CUP FROM CAPTAIN WERNER ZAHN OF THE GERMAN BOBSLED TEAM.

refused to compete at the 1936 Games because they were held in Germany and he opposed that nation's Nazi leader, Adolf Hitler. When World War II broke out in Europe, Fiske joined Great Britain's Royal Air Force as a fighter pilot. He was severely injured in a dogfight with a German squadron on August 16, 1940, and died the next day. Just 29 years old, Fiske was the first American pilot to be killed in action during World War II.

As the Winter Games expanded their programs after the war, dominant athletes emerged who swept all the gold medals in their sports. First among them in Alpine skiing was Anton "Toni" Sailer of Austria. Sailer started the 1956 Winter Games by winning the giant slalom by 6.2 seconds, still the largest margin of victory in an Olympic Alpine race. He followed two days later by taking the gold in the slalom by four seconds. Three days after that he was about to start his run in the downhill when the strap that held one of his boots to his ski broke. Fortunately, the trainer of the Italian team volunteered the strap from his own ski, and Sailer was able to compete. He raced down the course 3.5 seconds faster than anyone else and had Alpine skiing's first Olympic triple crown. The sweep "elevated him to the stature of the other athletic giants who at one time ruled the world," wrote a *New York Times* reporter, referring to Sailer as a "bronzed 20-year-old Austrian" who "looks

STILL CLUTCHING HIS SKI POLES,
ANTON "TONI" SAILER POSES
FOR A PHOTOGRAPH AFTER
WINNING HIS THIRD GOLD MEDAL
AT CORTINA D'AMPEZZO IN 1956.

like a movie star and skis like a dream." After the Olympics, Sailer did go on to become a movie star in Europe and Asia, as well as a recording artist and the coach of the Austrian ski team.

In 1964, speed skater Lydia Skoblikova dominated her sport and set an all-time Winter Games record as well. The 24-year-old teacher from the Siberia region of the Soviet Union charmed the media with her sparkling blue eyes and dimpled cheeks, but she was all business on the ice. On four straight days, she won gold medals in the 500-, 1,500-, 1,000-, and 3,000-meter speed skating races. That made her the first athlete to win four gold medals at a single Winter Olympiad and the first to win four gold medals in individual events at any Olympiad, winter or summer. With her two golds from the 1960 Games, Skoblikova remains the only woman to win six gold medals in individual events at the Winter Olympics.

While Skoblikova's performance was proof of the growing dominance of the Soviet Union in a number of sports, the U.S. was developing a reputation as a powerhouse in the individual figure skating events. U.S. men won the gold medal at every Olympics from 1948 through 1960, and U.S. women won in 1956 and 1960. Although many of the nation's top skaters retired after the 1960 Games, the outlook for a new crop of champions was good. On February 13, 1961, *Sports Illustrated* featured the top female prospect, 16-year-old Laurence Owen, on the cover. Owen was the sister of pairs skater Maribel Owen and the daughter of 1932 bronze medalist Maribel Vinson Owen, who had coached 1956 Olympic champion Tenley Albright. Now her mother hoped to coach both daughters to medals of their own. But just two days after *Sports Illustrated* shined the spotlight on Laurence and her family, tragedy struck. An airplane carrying the three

Owen women and the entire 1961 U.S. figure skating team crashed in Belgium, killing all 72 people on board. Among the dead were 18 skaters as well as many coaches, officials, and family members.

With a generation of skaters lost, the U.S. team struggled to rebuild. At the 1964 Winter Games U.S. skaters won only a single medal, a bronze in the men's event by Scott Allen. But a surprising entry on the women's side gave the U.S. hope for a brighter future. Peggy Fleming had been only 12 years old at the time of the tragic plane crash, but her coach, Bill Kipp, was among those who perished. After Kipp's death Fleming went through a series of coaches, but still managed to win the U.S. senior national title at 15 to make it onto the Olympic team. She placed sixth at the Olympics in 1964 and continued to improve. By the time the 1968 Winter Games came along, Fleming had won the U.S. national title five times in a row and the world title twice. She capped her accomplishments and ushered in a new era of figure skating by winning the 1968 Olympic gold medal in a performance that was shown on TV around the world.

Television cameras also followed the success of Alpine skier Jean-Claude Killy at the 1968 Winter Games. The handsome Frenchman thrilled the crowd as well as TV viewers when he snatched the gold medal in the downhill by only eight-hundredths of a second. He won the giant slalom four days later, and it looked like he might repeat Toni Sailer's sweep of the Alpine events. When it was time for

Scott Allen and Peggy Fleming, above, helped revive the U.S. figure skating program in 1964. Below, a copy of Sports Illustrated in the wreckage of the 1961 plane crash.

Killy's last race, the slalom, the course was shrouded in fog. Killy managed to clock the fastest time during the first of two runs, and he led off the second round with a strong showing. Then the fog thickened and several skiers fell or missed gates. Karl Schranz of Austria stopped skiing only a third of the way down the course because he claimed someone had darted in front of him. He was granted a rerun and completed the race fast enough to win the gold. But a jury of appeal found that Schranz had missed two gates on his original run before any interference had taken place. He was disqualified and Killy was awarded his third gold medal. With his triple victory, Killy became a hero whose success encouraged people around the world to take to the slopes.

Speed skating has never been a mainstream sport in the United States, and that's just the way Wisconsin-born Eric Heiden liked it. In the late 1970s, Heiden was so popular in Europe that a song about him, "The Ballad of Eric Heiden," was a big hit in Norway. But few people in the U.S. knew who he was. That changed at the 1980 Winter Games, held in Lake Placid, New York. Over the course of nine days, Heiden earned gold medals in all five of the speed skating events on the program, setting four Olympic records and one world record along the way. He was the first winter or summer athlete to win five individual gold medals at a single Olympics and he remains the only Winter Olympian ever to earn five gold medals in one year. But Heiden quit competitive skating soon after Lake Placid. "Maybe if things had stayed the way they were and I could still be obscure....I might want to keep skating," he said. "I really liked it best when I was a nobody."

When reporters asked Eric Heiden to name the greatest moment of the 1980 Winter Games, he answered, "That's simple....when the United States

JEAN-CLAUDE KILLY NEGOTIATES THE GATES IN THE CONTROVERSIAL SLALOM RACE AT THE 1968 WINTER GAMES. KILLY LATER BECAME A MEMBER OF THE INTERNATIONAL OLYMPIC COMMITTEE AND WAS INSTRUMENTAL IN HELPING TO ORGANIZE THE 1992, 1998, 2002, AND 2006 WINTER OLYMPICS.

beat the Russians in the hockey game." The U.S. ice hockey team's road to the 1980 gold medal—and particularly the win against the Soviet Union—was such a dramatic story of underdogs succeeding against all odds that the media dubbed it the "Miracle on Ice." But it was even more remarkable because the U.S. had pulled off a surprisingly similar victory 20 years before. In 1960, as in 1980, the Winter Games took place in the United States. Both times the U.S. hockey team was a ragtag group of college and club players that hadn't shown much promise before the Olympics. The 1960 squad, later nicknamed the "Team of Destiny," surprised most observers by winning their first five games and then beating the Soviet Union and Czechoslovakia to take the gold. That last win, wrote the *New York Times*, "capped one of the finest showings by any squad since the first winter games at Chamonix."

Eric Heiden sprints to his first gold medal and a new Olympic record in the 500-meter speed skating race at Lake Placid. After winning an unprecedented five gold medals in 1980, Heiden turned to cycling, racing professionally for several years. He also followed in his father's footsteps and went to medical school to become an orthopedic surgeon. At the 2002 Olympics, he served as doctor for the U.S. speed skating team.

MEMBERS OF THE U.S. ICE HOCKEY TEAM REJOICE AFTER THEIR VICTORY OVER THE SOVIET UNION ON FEBRUARY 20, 1980. GOALTENDER JIM CRAIG TALLIED 39 SAVES AS TEAMMATES MARK JOHNSON AND MIKE ERUZIONE NETTED CLUTCH SHOTS TO ENSURE THE UPSET THAT WAS QUICKLY DUBBED THE "MIRACLE ON ICE." THE TEAM'S QUEST FOR THE GOLD MEDAL WAS DRAMATIZED IN THE 2004 FEATURE FILM *MIRACLE.*

In 1960 Herb Brooks was the last player to be cut from the U.S. hockey team. Twenty years later Brooks was the coach of the U.S. team. One of the men on his squad was Dave Christian, son of 1960 star Billy Christian. Again the U.S. was undefeated in its first five games, winning four and tying one. And again the Americans faced the Soviet Union in the first game of the medal round. When the U.S. beat the mighty Soviets 4–3, the victory set off joyous celebrations in Lake Placid and across the country. Two days later, the U.S. clinched the gold by beating Finland 2–1, but it was the win over the Soviets that thrilled fans the most. President Jimmy Carter had threatened a U.S. boycott of the 1980 Summer Olympics, which were to be held in the Soviet Union, as a protest against the Soviets' invasion of Afghanistan. The U.S. defeat of the Soviets in the hockey arena seemed to strengthen the spirit of a nation that was divided over the Olympic boycott and worried about the future. The symbolic "Miracle on Ice" could not have come at a better time.

Just as the Soviets were a force to be reckoned with in ice hockey, they quickly became dominant in the relatively new sport of ice dancing. This figure skating event, first contested at the 1976 Winter Games, requires partners to dance on ice, performing routines that are more fluid and less gymnastic than those in pairs skating. Soviet skaters won the ice dancing gold medals in both 1976 and 1980, but in 1984 a couple emerged who elevated the sport to a whole new level. Great Britain's Jayne Torvill and Christopher Dean started skating together in 1975, and by 1984 they had perfected an elegant, romantic style in routines choreographed by Dean. On Valentine's Day, 1984, they performed a dance to Maurice Ravel's classical piece "Bolero" that stunned audiences with its beauty. All nine of the judges awarded Torvill and Dean perfect 6.0 scores for artistic impression and TV commentator Dick Button called the performance "the most beautiful and emotional moment I have ever experienced." Torvill and Dean left the amateur ranks after the 1984 Games, but returned to the Olympics in 1994, when the rules were changed to allow professional skaters. That year they won the bronze medal in a controversial outcome in which the judges failed to penalize the winning Russian couple for several obvious violations.

At the same time that Torvill and Dean were filling figure skating audiences with awe, two U.S. speed skaters won the admiration of fans with their persistence and dedication. Bonnie Blair entered her first Winter Games as a 19-year-old in 1984, finishing eighth in her only race, the 500 meters. She continued to train and improve, buoyed by the "Blair Bunch," a strong and ever-growing group of family and friends who traveled to her competitions. At the 1988 Games in Calgary, Blair beat favorite Christa Rothenburger to

ICE DANCERS TORVILL AND DEAN PERFORM THE MAGICAL ROUTINE THAT WON THEM THE GOLD MEDAL IN 1984.

BONNIE BLAIR HEADS TOWARD HER SECOND GOLD MEDAL OF THE ALBERTVILLE GAMES AS SHE FINISHES THE 1,000-METER RACE.

DAN JANSEN HOLDS HIS DAUGHTER JANE AFTER WINNING IN 1994.

RAISA SMETANINA JOKES THAT SINCE HER FEBRUARY 29 BIRTHDAY COMES ALONG ONLY IN LEAP YEARS, SHE WAS REALLY ONLY 10 WHEN SHE WON HER FINAL GOLD MEDAL.

take the gold in the 500 meters and also won the bronze in the 1,000. In 1992, Blair earned gold medals in both of those events, and she did the same in 1994. By doing so, this modest athlete from Champaign, Illinois, became the first speed skater of either gender to win the same event three times in a row and the first American to win six medals at the Winter Games.

Meanwhile one of Blair's teammates, Dan Jansen, showed his strength of character by refusing to give up. A sprinter like Blair, the Wisconsin native also skated at the Winter Games for the first time in 1984, finishing out of medal contention. By 1988 Jansen was a favorite in both the 500 and the 1,000 meters, but he arrived in Calgary with a heavy heart. His older sister Jane was battling leukemia, and on the day of the 500, she died. At his family's urging, Jansen entered the race, only to fall in the first turn. Four days later, he also fell in the 1,000. Jansen went to Albertville in 1992, but again he failed to medal. He decided to try once more in Lillehammer. Though a slip dashed his medal hopes in the 500, Jansen skated magnificently in the 1,000, setting a world record and winning the gold. He accepted the medal with tears in his eyes and then took a victory lap holding his baby daughter, who he'd named after his sister Jane.

In the sport of cross country skiing, where endurance is key, no one proved that she could go the distance better than Raisa Smetanina. Skiing for the Soviet Union, Smetanina appeared in her first Winter Games in 1976. She returned in 1980, 1984, 1988, and 1992 and won a total of four gold medals, five silver medals, and one bronze. Smetanina is the only athlete to medal at five consecutive Winter Olympiads and the only female winter athlete to win a total of ten medals. She is also the oldest female

An exhausted Bjørn Dæhlie remained on the ground for five minutes after throwing himself over the finish line in his last Olympic race, the 50-kilometer at Nagano. Dæhlie skied for over two hours to eke out an 8.1-second victory over Niklas Jonsson of Sweden. The win gave Dæhlie his 12th medal overall and tied him with Lydia Skoblikova as the only Winter Olympians to win six gold medals in individual events.

Winter Olympics gold medalist ever, having won her last medal just ten days before her 40th birthday.

Bjørn Dæhlie of Norway was even more successful in the cross country ranks. Dæhlie, who competed in 1992, 1994, and 1998, is the most decorated athlete in the history of the Winter Games. His eight gold medals and 12 total medals were earned skiing distances from 10 kilometers to 50 kilometers and taking part in the men's 4 x 10-kilometer relay. Dæhlie was forced to retire a few months before the 2002 Winter Games due to back problems, but his legacy lives on. A British reporter wrote in 2002, "In Norwegian eyes, there will never be a winter Olympian to rival Dæhlie."

★ Jim Shea ★ of the U.S. temporarily soars above his sled as he leaves the gate in the 2002 skeleton final. Shea, a third-generation Winter Olympian, would take the gold.

In 1998, freestyle skier ★ Xu Nannan ★ of China seems to reach the clouds in her qualifying jump during the women's aerials. Xu would go on to win the silver medal behind Nikki Stone of the U.S.

★ Hiroki Yamada ★ of Japan sails through the air during a practice session a day before the start of the 2002 Winter Games.

★ Franco Cavegn ★ of Switzerland is airborne during the men's downhill at Nagano. Cavegn would finish out of medal contention.

★ Birger Ruud ★ seems suspended over the crowd during his gold medal–winning ski jump in 1936. The Norwegian already had won the event in 1932 and would return in 1948 to add a silver medal to his collection.

★ **Jeanette Altwegg** ★ of Great Britain leaps across the ice on the way to a gold medal in the women's figure skating competition at the 1952 Winter Games.

★ **Deidra Dionne** ★ of Canada spins upside down in the finals of the women's aerials in 2002. Dionne would win the bronze medal.

Ski goggles
circa 1920

SOARING

★ **Markku Koski** ★ of Finland catches air during the qualifying round of the halfpipe snowboarding competition at Salt Lake City. Koski would finish eighth.

Norway's ★ **Torbjørn Yggeseth** ★ goes all out at the 1964 Winter Games. After competing in two Olympics, Yggeseth would become an international ski jump official.

Three days after Nancy Kerrigan, right, was attacked by men with ties to Tonya Harding, left, the two skaters sit next to each other as they pose for a photograph of the 1994 U.S. Olympic figure skating team. Top, a pair of vintage figure skates from the collection of the International Olympic Committee.

On February 23, 1994, close to 46 million people in the United States and countless others around the world sat in front of their television sets watching the most highly anticipated battle of the 17th Olympic Winter Games. They weren't anxiously following a politically charged hockey match or a series of death-defying ski runs. Instead, they were engrossed in the rather serene action of the short program in

INTIMATE
CONFLICTS

women's figure skating. As one skater after another made her way through the eight required elements, everyone waited for the two Americans who had dominated newspaper headlines for weeks. Finally, a skater in a bright red costume glided across the ice. Tonya Harding, the reigning U.S. figure skating champion, had arrived.

Just seven weeks before, Harding's rival, Nancy Kerrigan, had been attacked and injured by men with ties to Harding. Now, as the two women went head-to-head at the Olympics, skating fans and tabloid readers alike tuned in to see how the continuing drama would play out. The events involving Harding and Kerrigan were the most extreme example of the scandals and controversies that occasionally

have overshadowed the more inspirational stories of the Winter Olympics. The cozy nature of the Winter Games seems to produce conflicts that are more intimate and personal than those at Summer Olympiads. Athletes' rivalries, struggles over amateurism, and judging irregularities have cast specific individuals as heroes or villains. At times, the furor over some of these issues has been so severe that the very future of the Winter Games has been in jeopardy.

While the Harding-Kerrigan affair did not threaten to derail the Games altogether, it did reflect how commercialized the Winter Olympics had become and how much pressure some athletes put on themselves to win. Both Tonya Harding and Nancy Kerrigan had been rising young stars when Harding won a gold medal at the U.S. Figure Skating Championships in 1991. But since then Kerrigan had earned more accolades. She'd won a bronze medal at the 1992 Winter Olympics and a gold medal at the 1993 U.S. Championships. Harding, who had grown up in difficult circumstances and married young, began to resent Kerrigan's success and her image as an "All-American girl." She watched enviously as Kerrigan got commercial endorsements from Coca-Cola, Reebok, Campbell's soup, and several other sponsors. To earn sympathy, Harding went so far as to have an anonymous death threat against herself sent to officials at one U.S. skating tournament. After learning about the threat, New York Yankees owner George Steinbrenner sent Harding $20,000 to help pay her training expenses.

Harding's fabricated death threat was followed by an even more drastic act. On January 6, 1994, both Harding and Kerrigan were in Detroit, Michigan, to compete in the 1994 U.S. Championships, whose winner and runner-up would go on to the Lillehammer Olympics. Soon after Kerrigan finished a practice session, a man approached her from behind and whacked her right leg with a metal baton, striking it just above the knee. Kerrigan collapsed in agony and had no choice but to withdraw from the tournament, which Harding went on to win. Within a few weeks, Harding's former husband, Jeff Gillooly, as well as her bodyguard and two other men were arrested for the attack. Gillooly said Harding knew about his plan and had gathered information for him about Kerrigan's training schedule. When officials of the U.S. Olympic Committee (USOC) heard about Harding's alleged involvement, they threatened to ban her from the Winter Games. Harding responded by suing the USOC for interfering with her right to compete. In the end, the USOC backed down. Meanwhile Kerrigan quickly recovered from her injuries and was given a place on the U.S. team.

Ultimately, even the desperate measures taken by Harding's supporters could not help her win an Olympic medal. "Harding blew her medal hopes in only 30 seconds," remembers Olympic historian David Wallechinsky. "She double-footed the landing of her first triple jump, took extra steps during a combo and even double-footed a relatively easy double flip." Harding was in tenth place following the short program, and two days later she showed up so late for the

DURING THE FREE SKATE KERRIGAN, ABOVE, SHOWS HER BALLETIC STYLE WHILE HARDING, BELOW, COMPLAINS ABOUT HER BOOT LACE.

long program, or free skate, that she nearly was disqualified. After a shaky start, she stopped skating only 45 seconds into her four-minute routine because of a problem with her boot lace. She was allowed to begin again and succeeded in pulling herself up to eighth place. Meanwhile, Kerrigan had skated a clean short program and went into the next round in first place. Though her free skate was nearly flawless, 16-year-old Oksana Baiul of Ukraine came from behind to edge out Kerrigan for the gold.

Following the 1994 Olympics, Jeff Gillooly admitted his guilt and was fined $100,000 and sentenced to two years in prison, while his three associates were sentenced to 18 months each. Harding pleaded guilty to hindering the prosecution of the case and was fined $100,000 and sentenced to three years of probation and 500 hours of community service. The U.S. Figure Skating Association stripped Harding of her 1994 championship title and banned her for life from competing in their events or coaching their skaters. Harding continued to have trouble after that, marrying and divorcing again and getting into scrapes that sometimes involved police intervention. Kerrigan's life after Lillehammer was a much calmer mixture of endorsements, charity work, marriage and motherhood, and some skating.

There were no physical attacks on athletes in the controversy over the amateur status of downhill skiers, but the battle lasted 40 years and put an end to the career of at least one Olympian. The problem dated back to the founding of the modern Olympic Games in 1894. One of the central components of the Games was that they would be open only to amateur athletes who competed for the love of sport, rather than for financial gain. Coaches or instructors who earned a salary could not compete, nor could anyone else who was paid for

playing any sport or awarded money for winning any athletic event. This policy caused particular difficulties when Alpine skiing was added to the program of the Winter Games in 1936. At the time, Alpine was a relatively new form of recreation, and many ski resorts hired the best skiers as instructors to help tourists develop their skills. Based on IOC policies, those instructors were not eligible to compete in the Olympics. But the international group that governed Alpine skiing events, the Fédération Internationale de Ski (FIS), would not accept that without a fight.

FIS rules held that teachers of a sport should not be considered professionals in that sport, but the IOC vehemently disagreed. The FIS gave in for 1936, but declared that skiers would compete only under FIS rules at the next Olympics. In turn, the IOC considered three options for the Winter Games in 1940, each more extreme than the last. One was to hold the 1940 Games without skiing competitions. The second was to cancel the 1940 Games. The third was to discontinue the Winter Olympics forever. IOC members agreed on the first option, but then ended up canceling the 1940 Games because World War II made it impossible to hold them. When the Olympic schedule resumed after the war, the IOC and FIS

IOC PRESIDENT AVERY BRUNDAGE, ABOVE, HAD NO TOLERANCE FOR ATHLETES WHO HE FELT VIOLATED THE OLYMPIC RULES ON AMATEURISM. JEAN-CLAUDE KILLY, BELOW, FOUND WAYS TO PUSH THE ENVELOPE.

reached a compromise. Ski instructors would be allowed to compete in the 1948 Winter Games as long as they did not accept payment for their services after October 1, 1946. This temporarily appeased both sides and the IOC expanded the 1948 Olympic Alpine program to three events for men and three for women. But the fight over amateurism in skiing was far from over. A new IOC president would take it to a whole new level.

Avery Brundage was an American who had earned his fortune in real estate and construction. He had represented the U.S. in the decathlon at the 1912 Summer Olympics and had been involved in the Olympic Movement ever since. In 1952, Brundage became president of the IOC, preaching a fierce dedication to amateurism at the Olympics. "The Olympic Games are and must remain amateur or they cannot exist," he wrote in 1957. A decade later he had not changed his opinion. "We have heard much of the complicated amateur problem," he said. "Despite all the talk, it is not complicated at all. The Games are not commercial. They are not a business and those whose aim is to make money from sport are not wanted. It is as simple as that."

However, saying it was simple didn't make it so. By the late 1960s, the line between amateurs and professionals in sports was becoming more and more blurred. Pros and amateurs competed side by side in "open" tennis and golf tournaments. Athletes in Communist countries were paid as "government employees," which allowed them to play their sports full-time but still be considered amateurs. And in skiing, manufacturers gladly donated skis, boots, and gloves to Olympic athletes so their logos would be seen on TV. Although it was hard to prove, Avery Brundage was certain that manufacturers also secretly paid skiers to use their equipment. This so enraged him that he called Alpine skiing "a poisonous tumor to be immediately operated on." His solution in 1968 was to assign someone to snatch the equipment from skiers as soon as they finished their races so they could not show off the manufacturer's logos. But clever athletes found ways to get their message across. Jean-Claude Killy, the winner of three gold medals in 1968, had a friend in the crowd who ran to embrace him at the end of his downhill run. Though Killy's skis were confiscated, his friend carried his own pair, made by the same company, which he held close to Killy when photographs were taken.

By 1972, Brundage had had enough. As the Winter Games in Sapporo, Japan, approached, he stated that he would ban ten skiers who reportedly had been paid to take part in an event in the U.S. He backed down after six countries threatened to boycott the Olympics and instead focused his efforts on one man. Karl Schranz of Austria already had courted controversy when he was disqualified after missing gates in a foggy slalom race at the 1968 Games. Now Brundage declared that he was ineligible for the 1972 Games because he had allowed his name and picture to be used in numerous advertisements. Schranz was suspected of earning as much as $50,000 a year designing and testing ski products. He responded to the ban by blasting Brundage and the concept of amateurism. "If Mr. Brundage had been poor, as I once was and as were many other athletes, I wonder if he wouldn't have a different attitude," said Schranz. "If his recommendations were followed, then the Olympics would be a competition only for the rich. No man of ordinary means could ever afford to excel in his sport....The Olympic Games should be a competition of skill and strength and speed—no more."

Brundage retired from the presidency of the IOC later in 1972, but he took a parting shot at Alpine skiers and the Winter Games in general. "A serious mistake was made when the Olympic Winter Games were founded," he declared at his last IOC meeting. Looking ahead to the next Winter Olympiad, slated for Denver, Colorado, he added, "May [the Winter Olympics] receive an honorable funeral in Denver." But the 1976 Games never made it to Colorado. Denver's citizens rejected them and the town of Innsbruck, Austria, stepped in as host. And rather than pulling the plug on the Winter Olympics, the IOC instead eased up on the amateur rules. In 1981, the IOC gave the responsibility of deciding who was eligible to compete to the international federation that governs each Olympic sport. Most, including the FIS, were quick to allow professionals into the Games.

Officials were at the center of two additional scandals as the Olympics approached and entered the 21st century. The first one broke in November 1998, when evidence surfaced that the Salt Lake City Organizing Committee (SLOC) had been paying the college tuition of an IOC member's daughter in exchange for his vote to bring the 2002 Winter Games to Utah. Further investigation showed that the SLOC had given gifts and scholarships to a number of IOC members and had even paid for medical treatments and vacations for members and their families. One delegate alone received $300,000 worth of gifts and services, only to tell the investigators who accused him of taking bribes that such arrangements were "normal." In fact, IOC member Marc Hodler, who first raised the allegations of bribery, charged that the practice dated as far back as 1990, when Atlanta, Georgia, was chosen to host the 1996 Summer Olympics.

U.S. and Olympic officials launched no fewer than four separate investigations into the bribery charges, and in the end, 19 members of the IOC and several SLOC members resigned or were expelled. Beyond that, in December 1999, the IOC instituted wholesale reforms in how it chooses sites for the Summer and Winter Games. The new procedures prohibit most IOC members from visiting candidate cities. Instead, they rely on the efforts of an evaluation commission made up of IOC members, athletes, and representatives of various sports federations and national Olympic committees. Once the evaluation commission has done the legwork, it submits a report and all 130-plus members of the IOC take part in the final vote. Another new regulation closely monitors gifts given to IOC members.

Salt Lake City recovered from the bribery scandal, but the opening days of the 2002 Winter Games saw yet another incident that would have far-reaching effects. The setting, once again, was figure skating, but this time the trouble centered on the judges. On Monday, February 11, Canadian pairs skaters Jamie Salé and David Pelletier captivated the crowd at the Salt Lake Ice Center with a flawless free skate, only to finish second in the judges' rankings to the less-than-perfect pair from Russia, Elena Berezhnaya and Anton Sikharulidze. The audience responded to the results with waves of jeers that were echoed by TV commentators and later by the press. The Canadians so obviously had given the better performance that the IOC pressured the International Skating Union (ISU) to look for scoring irregularities. Within 24 hours the French judge, Marie Reine Le Gougne, admitted that the head of the French Skating Federation had pressured her to vote for the Russians. Her vote tipped the results in the Russians' favor, 5 to 4, giving them the gold medal.

Canadians Jamie Salé and David Pelletier perform their poetic free skate performance in the finals of the pairs competition in Salt Lake City, above, only to be shocked when they learn that their scores are not good enough to win the gold, below. With them is their coach, Jan Ullmark.

Before more sophisticated means of reporting the scores at figure skating competitions were introduced, judges at the Winter Games stood on the ice holding up cards that indicated the points they awarded each athlete. They gave each skater two scores of 0 to 6, one for technical merit and the other for artistic impression. The judges shown here are evaluating a performance at the 1936 Olympics.

By the end of the week, the ISU had suspended Le Gougne and awarded Salé and Pelletier a duplicate pair of gold medals. But the investigation continued. In late July, a Russian man with a history of criminal activity was arrested as the person behind the judging scandal. It seemed that the man, Alimzhan Tokhtakhounov, had worked with an official from the Russian Skating Federation to fix the results of not one, but two skating contests in Salt Lake City. First they made sure that the Russians won the pairs competition. Then they delivered the victory in ice dancing to Marina Anissina and Gwendal Peizerat, the couple from France. Tokhtakhounov hoped his efforts would convince his friends in France to help him obtain a visa that would permit him to live in that country. Instead, he was arrested and charged with bribery and fraud.

While the 2002 judging scandal was extreme, it came after more than 80 years of questionable calls that some skaters had grown to expect. As early as 1920, when figure skating was contested at the Summer Olympics, Theresa Weld of the U.S. charged that skating judges were "unavoidably prejudiced" in favor of citizens of their own nations. In 1938, sportswriter Paul Gallico called figure skating, "for the most part as completely and joyously crooked and bought and sold as any prizefight or wrestling championship." The artistic nature of figure skating makes it impossible to determine the outcome of an event with a stopwatch, as in skiing, or a tape measure, as in ski jumping. Instead, it is up to figure skating judges to watch a performance and grade it based on technical and artistic merit. For over a century, judges based their grades on a system where 6.0 was the highest mark that could be given. After awarding each skater technical and artistic grades of 6.0 or less, they would rank the skaters against each other. Nine judges could watch the same performances and each come up with completely different rankings. Sometimes they let the skaters' nationalities or reputations influence their votes. But often, they just saw the performances differently.

After 2002, the ISU decided to scrap their old judging system in favor of a more objective—and more complex—computer-based approach. Now a Technical Specialist watches each performance and dictates the possible point value of each element, such as a jump or spin, which the judges then grade. Judges also score the quality of five program components: skating skills, transitions, execution, choreography, and interpretation. Nine judges are randomly chosen from a panel of 12 to grade a competition, and the highest and lowest scores for each skater are deleted. The seven remaining numbers are averaged to get the skater's final score. This new system, first used in 2004, tends to reward the skaters whose programs have a higher degree of difficulty. Whether it solves the problems that have plagued Olympic figure skating since the beginning still remains to be seen.

PAIRS JUDGE MARIE REINE LE GOUGNE OF FRANCE APPEARS AT A PRESS CONFERENCE AFTER ADMITTING HER PART IN THE JUDGING SCANDAL AT SALT LAKE CITY.

At the 2002 Winter Games, U.S. snowboarders would finish in four of the top six slots in the halfpipe competition. Tommy Czeschin, shown here, was third after the first heat but would end up in sixth place. Top, one of the earliest Snurfers, the 1960s snowboards built with a rope attached for steering and sold for $15 apiece.

BEFORE THE 2002 WINTER GAMES, only one threesome of U.S. athletes ever had swept the gold, silver, and bronze Olympic medals in a single winter event. Hayes Alan Jenkins, Ronald Robertson, and David Jenkins had finished first, second, and third, respectively, in figure skating in 1956, earning their victories performing to the flowing chords of classical music. Forty-six years later, another U.S. threesome

GOING TO
EXTREMES

finished one-two-three as the pounding beat of Metallica, AC/DC, and Black Sabbath filled the air. Snowboarders Ross Powers, Danny Kass, and J. J. Thomas dominated the halfpipe and made it clear that the Winter Games had entered a new era.

Snowboarding hadn't even been invented when the Jenkins brothers and Robertson starred at Cortina d'Ampezzo. It wasn't until 1965 that a Michigan man connected two skis side by side to built a "Snurfer" so his daughters could while away the winter surfing on the snow. By the early 1980s, manufacturers were making boards with bindings that held a rider's feet in place and calling them snowboards instead of Snurfers. And although most ski areas prohibited the sport, it

SHANNON BAHRKE OF THE U.S. GIVES IT HER ALL IN THE FINALS OF THE FREESTYLE SKIING MOGULS CONTEST AT THE SALT LAKE CITY GAMES. BAHRKE WOULD FINISH WITH A SILVER MEDAL WHILE KARI TRAA OF NORWAY, THE BRONZE MEDALIST AT NAGANO, WOULD TAKE THE GOLD.

continued to gain momentum, especially with young people. In 1994, the National Sporting Goods Association reported that there were 2.1 million snowboarders in the U.S. alone, and 55 percent of them were under age 17. When the International Olympic Committee started searching for new "extreme" sports that would attract a younger crowd of spectators to the Winter Games, snowboarding was a natural choice.

Yet snowboarding wasn't the first new sport added to the Winter Games in an effort to appeal to a broader audience. In 1988, freestyle skiing had its debut as a non-medal sport in Calgary. Athletes demonstrated three disciplines of freestyle skiing, all of which combine Alpine skiing and acrobatics. In the moguls (bumps), athletes ski down a bumpy course and perform two jumps along the way. They are judged on the quality of their turns, their aerial maneuvers, and their speed. In freestyle skiing, competitors launch themselves into two different jumps, during which they do a combination of somersaults and twists before landing on a steep hill. They are judged on their takeoffs, their form in the air, and their landings. In ski ballet—later renamed Acroski—athletes perform a downhill run with jumps and spins that is choreographed to music. They receive scores for technical difficulty and artistic impression. IOC officials voted to add the moguls to the Olympic program as a medal sport in 1992 and to add freestyle skiing in 1994.

Short track speed skating also premiered as a demonstration sport in 1988 and as a medal sport at the 1992 Winter Games. In short track, athletes race on an oval that is about one-quarter the size of the oval used in traditional long track speed skating. While in long track men and women race in pairs against the clock, in short track they race in packs of four or more skaters, and the first skater to cross the finish line wins. Short track skaters must jockey for position without pushing or bumping their opponents or making body contact of any kind. Athletes compete in single events or team relays. In 1992, the IOC introduced four events: the 1,000 meters and the 5,000-meter relay for men and the 500 meters and 3,000-meter relay for women. By 2002, they had added two more individual events to both the men's and women's programs.

As freestyle skiing and short track speed skating carved out a place at the Winter Olympics, the visibility of snowboarding got a boost with the 1997 premier of the Winter X Games. Created by the ESPN cable TV networks, the Winter X Games aimed to capitalize on the "sheer unadulterated athletic lunacy" that the Summer X Games had been celebrating since 1995.

TRAVIS MAYLER OF THE U.S. PRACTICES ON THE MOGULS COURSE AT THE 2002 WINTER GAMES. A FEW DAYS LATER, MAYLER WOULD WIN THE SILVER MEDAL.

In one of the most dramatic events at the 2002 Winter Games, Apolo Anton Ohno of the U.S. leads the pack during the men's 1,000-meter short track speed skating race. Before the race was over, Ohno and the rest of the leaders would collide, allowing the last-place skater, Australia's Steven Bradbury, to pass them all and win. Ohno would pick himself up and lunge over the finish line for the silver medal, while Mathieu Turcotte of Canada would win the bronze. Ohno would also win a gold medal in the 1,500-meter race after the first-place finisher was disqualified for interference.

The first winter edition featured ice climbing, snow mountain bike racing, "super-modified shovel racing," snowboarding, and other youth-oriented extreme sports. Held in Big Bear Lake, California, they were broadcast in 21 different languages and televised in 198 countries and territories. The Winter X Games have continued on an annual basis, with new events added almost every year.

Snowboarding made the leap to the Olympic Winter Games in 1998, although some of the independent spirits in the sport were uncomfortable with the idea of competition. "Snowboarding is all about free riding and individuality," said U.S. rider Michelle Taggart. "You try for the most perfect run, and you ought to be happy just knowing you did your best." Added Ross Powers, "We aren't really into rivalries. We're just going to go out and rip through the powder, just like we would on any mountain, at any time." While Taggart and Powers went to the Nagano Games, one of the top men in the sport didn't. "Snowboarding is about fresh tracks and carving powder and being yourself," said Terje Håkonsen of Norway, who boycotted the Games. "It's not about nationalism and politics and big money. Snowboarding is everything the Olympics isn't."

At Nagano, snowboarders competed in the half-pipe and the giant slalom, with separate events for men and women. In the halfpipe, snowboarders perform acrobatic tricks while riding up and down the walls of an icy trench that was dug deep into a hill. Five judges award them points for their maneuvers, rotations, height, speed, and overall performance. In giant slalom, athletes try to navigate a series of 40 to 50 gates on a hill as quickly as possible, much like the giant slalom event in Alpine skiing. However, since the 2002 Olympics, snowboarders have

SIX SNOWBOARDERS TAKE FLIGHT IN SNOWBOARD CROSS AT THE 2000 GOODWILL GAMES IN LAKE PLACID, NEW YORK. A REPORTER DESCRIBED THIS EVENT, ADDED TO THE WINTER GAMES IN 2006, AS "FOUR [TO SIX] SNOWBOARDERS REACHING SPEEDS OF 90 KILOMETERS PER HOUR IN A MAD DASH OVER A ROLLER-COASTER TRACK BOOBY-TRAPPED WITH SHARP CURVES, HUGE JUMPS AND DROPS THAT CAN THROW YOUR STOMACH INTO YOUR THROAT."

competed in the parallel giant slalom, with two riders going down parallel courses at the same time. The faster rider in each pair moves on to the next round.

After the 2002 Games in Salt Lake City, IOC president Jacques Rogge noted that it was his goal "to make sure we have sports that are popular, that attract the interest of youth." Television ratings for the Games in the U.S. were one sign that he was successful. Among 18- to 34-year-olds, viewership for the 2002 Winter Games was up 23 percent over the 1998 Games. Among males in that age category, the increase was 26 percent. When members of the IOC's Olympic Programme Commission met to consider new sports for the 2006 Winter Games, they took such statistics into consideration. "The Commission noted the high appeal for spectators and broadcast of the snowboard events in the Olympic Programmes of 1998 and 2002, in particular with the youth group of 15–25 year olds," they stated in their report. Therefore, they recommended that the IOC consider one additional snowboarding event, snowboard cross, for inclusion in 2006.

Called "just about the burliest comp[etition] on a snowboard" by the official Web site of the X Games, snowboard cross is also known as Snowboarder X and boardercross. In this event, groups of four to six riders compete at the same time, racing against each other to the finish line on a course with a variety of terrains and obstacles. Negotiating the moguls, banked turns, jumps, and drops while avoiding the other riders makes snowboard cross a treacherous sport, and even the top riders have suffered crashes and injuries. "Disaster lurks just about every moment," said Chris Klug, the 2002 Olympic bronze medalist in parallel giant slalom who broke his collarbone in snowboard cross at the 2005 Winter X Games. Added two-time U.S. champion Mark Schulz, "In any boardercross event, there's always one point where you're definitely not in control."

As the Winter Games embraced the extreme sports culture and added more perilous events to the program, at least one former Olympian expressed concern. "I worry about introducing some of these sports with a high risk factor," said speed skater Eric Heiden. An orthopedic surgeon who specializes in sports medicine, Heiden was particularly anxious about the aerials in freestyle skiing. In that event, competitors perform their somersaults and twists as high as 60 feet (18 meters) above the ground—three times the height reached by ski jumpers. "The consequences of a poor jumper are drastic," Heiden said. "I don't like to see sports where people risk their lives."

Despite these concerns, the future of the Winter Games seems to include sports where danger lurks at every turn. Among them is skeleton, the head-first sledding event that was reinstated at the 2002 Games after being contested in 1928 and 1948. "You definitely have to have some level of craziness to do our sport," said skeleton slider Tricia Stumpf, who missed the 2002 Olympics because of injuries. But the threat of danger seems to drive athletes to compete. "Nothing scares me more than going down a track at 80 miles per hour halfway out of control," said Jim Shea, Jr., the 2002 Olympic gold medalist in men's skeleton. "It's very exciting. I personally think it's one of the better sports."

Many athletes at the Olympic Winter Games seem to be driven as much by a desire to face their fears as to win medals. "That's your reward in the end," said U.S. Olympic snowboarder Tricia Byrnes, "when you overcome a fear or you do something that you didn't think you could do." In that respect, today's Winter Olympians aren't all that different from their predecessors. Norway's Birger Ruud, two-time gold medalist in ski jumping, reflected similar sentiments when he wrote about the Winter Games in 1945. "What do the Olympics mean to the individual?" asked Ruud. "Enjoyment and exhilaration for many, disappointment and too much sweat for others. However, everybody has the same aim: an objective which inspires us and makes us strong, and which requires self-discipline and sacrifice. Therefore, the Games are healthy and worthy competition for the world's youth."

TRICIA STUMPF COMES DOWN THE SKELETON TRACK DURING THE PARK CITY WORLD CUP IN FEBRUARY 2001, A TEST EVENT FOR THE 2002 WINTER GAMES.

★ **Vonetta Flowers** ★ of the U.S., right, hugs teammate ★ **Jill Bakken** ★ after they won the gold medal in the inaugural women's bobsled event in 2002. Flowers is the first black athlete ever to win a gold medal at the Winter Games.

Cross country skier ★ **Toini Gustafsson** ★ of Sweden gets a lift from her coach after winning her second gold medal at the 1968 Winter Games. She also would win a silver medal in the relay.

2002 Olympic
Gold Medal

★ **Team Belarus** ★ celebrates their upset victory over Sweden in the quarterfinals of the 2002 men's hockey tournament. Belarus would finish just out of medal contention.

★ **Anja Pärson** ★ of Sweden performs her patented victory slide after her second run in the women's slalom in 2002. Pärson would win a bronze medal in the slalom and a silver in the giant slalom.

★ **Tristan Gale** ★ of the U.S. catches snowflakes on her tongue after winning the gold medal in the first ever Olympic women's skeleton event in 2002.

South Korea's ★ **Choi Min-Kyung** ★ rejoices as her team wins the gold medal in the 3,000-meter short track speed skating relay in Salt Lake City.

CELEBRATING

★ **Georg Hackl** ★ of Germany thrusts his fist in the air after winning the silver medal in singles luge at the 2002 Winter Games. Hackl had won gold medals in the event at the three previous Olympics.

★ **Norwegian biathletes** ★ form a pyramid with skis and skiers after taking the gold medal in the 4 x 7.5-kilometer biathlon relay in 2002.

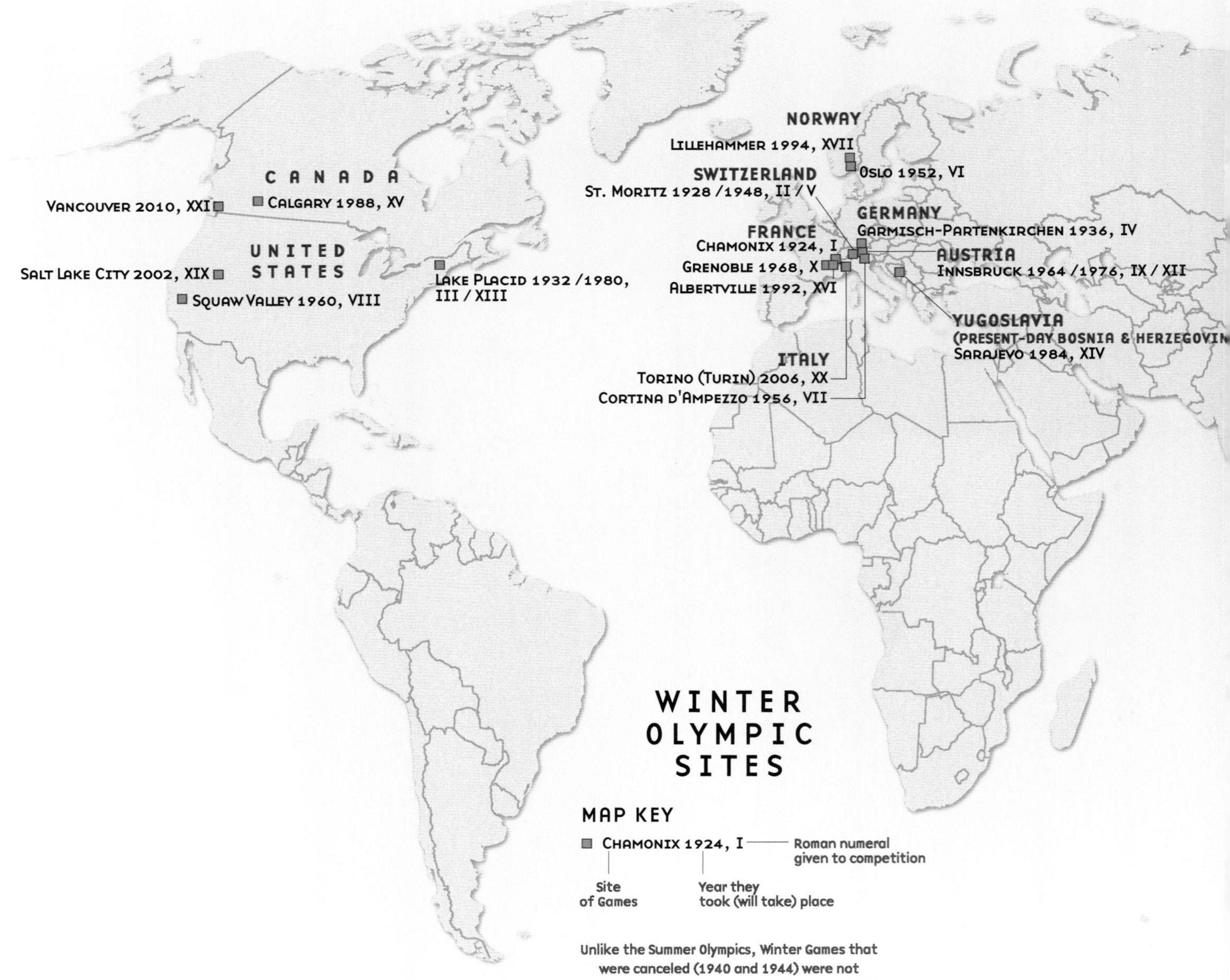

NORWAY
Lillehammer 1994, XVII
Oslo 1952, VI

SWITZERLAND
St. Moritz 1928/1948, II / V

GERMANY
Garmisch-Partenkirchen 1936, IV

FRANCE
Chamonix 1924, I
Grenoble 1968, X
Albertville 1992, XVI

AUSTRIA
Innsbruck 1964/1976, IX / XII

YUGOSLAVIA
(PRESENT-DAY BOSNIA & HERZEGOVIN
Sarajevo 1984, XIV

CANADA
Calgary 1988, XV
Vancouver 2010, XXI

UNITED
STATES
Salt Lake City 2002, XIX
Squaw Valley 1960, VIII
Lake Placid 1932/1980,
III / XIII

ITALY
Torino (Turin) 2006, XX
Cortina d'Ampezzo 1956, VII

WINTER OLYMPIC SITES

MAP KEY

Chamonix 1924, I ——— Roman numeral
given to competition

Site
of Games

Year they
took (will take) place

Unlike the Summer Olympics, Winter Games that
were canceled (1940 and 1944) were not
assigned Roman numerals. Therefore, the 1936
Winter Games were Winter Olympiad IV, while the
1948 Games were Winter Olympiad V.

Present-day country boundaries are shown.

Sapporo 1972, XI

JAPAN

Nagano 1998, XVIII

OLYMPIC
ALMANAC

WINTER OLYMPICS AT A GLANCE

No.	Year	Location	Nations	Sports	Events	Athletes	Male	Female
I	1924	CHAMONIX, FRANCE	16	6	16	258	247	11
II	1928	ST. MORITZ, SWITZERLAND	25	4	14	464	438	26
III	1932	LAKE PLACID, NEW YORK	17	4	14	252	231	21
IV	1936	GARMISCH-PARTENKIRCHEN, GERMANY	28	4	17	646	566	80
	1940				CANCELED			
	1944				CANCELED			
V	1948	ST. MORITZ, SWITZERLAND	28	4	22	669	592	77
VI	1952	OSLO, NORWAY	30	4	22	694	585	109
VII	1956	CORTINA D'AMPEZZO, ITALY	32	4	24	821	687	134
VIII	1960	SQUAW VALLEY, CALIFORNIA	30	4	27	665	521	144
IX	1964	INNSBRUCK, AUSTRIA	36	6	34	1,091	892	199
X	1968	GRENOBLE, FRANCE	37	6	35	1,158	947	211
XI	1972	SAPPORO, JAPAN	35	6	35	1,006	801	205
XII	1976	INNSBRUCK, AUSTRIA	37	6	37	1,123	892	231
XIII	1980	LAKE PLACID, NEW YORK	37	6	38	1,072	840	232
XIV	1984	SARAJEVO, YUGOSLAVIA*	49	6	39	1,272	998	274
XV	1988	CALGARY, CANADA	57	6	46	1,423	1,122	301
XVI	1992	ALBERTVILLE, FRANCE	64	7	57	1,801	1,313	488
XVII	1994	LILLEHAMMER, NORWAY	67	6	61	1,737	1,215	522
XVIII	1998	NAGANO, JAPAN	72	7	68	2,176	1,389	787
XIX	2002	SALT LAKE CITY, UTAH	77	7	78	2,399	1,513	886
XX	2006	TORINO, ITALY	80**	7	82**	2,550**		
XXI	2010	VANCOUVER, CANADA						

Note: Statistics in this table reflect those reported on the International Olympic Committee's official Web site, *www.olympics.org*. Due to inconsistent recordkeeping, some Olympic sources differ slightly on the numbers of male, female, and total athletes taking part in specific editions of the Winter Games.

*Now Bosnia & Herzegovina
**Estimate

ATHLETES FOR ALL SEASONS

To date, four athletes have won medals at both the Olympic Winter and Summer Games:

Athlete	Nation	Winter Sport / Year / Medal	Summer Sport / Year / Medal
Jacob Tullin Thams	Norway	Ski Jumping, 1924, gold	Yachting, 1936, silver
Eddie Eagan*	U.S.	Bobsled, 1932, gold	Boxing, 1920, gold
Christa Luding-Rothenburger**	East Germany	Speed Skating, 1984, gold; 1988, gold & silver; 1992, bronze	Cycling, 1988, silver
Clara Hughes	Canada	Speed Skating, 2002, bronze	Cycling, 1996, 2 bronze

*Only athlete to win gold medals in winter and summer
**Only athlete to win medals in the Winter and Summer Games the same year

YOUNGEST, OLDEST GOLD MEDALISTS

Age	Athlete	Achievement
13 years, 83 days	**Kim Yoon-mi** Korea Short Track Speed Skating	Youngest gold medalist ever (women's 3,000-meter relay, 1994)
15 years, 255 days	**Tara Lipinski** U.S. Figure Skating	Youngest gold medalist, individual event (ladies figure skating, 1998)
16 years, 259 days	**Toni Nieminen** Finland Ski Jumping	Youngest male gold medalist ever (large hill, team, 1992)
16 years, 261 days	**Toni Nieminen** Finland Ski Jumping	Youngest male gold medalist, individual event (large hill, individual, 1992)
33 years, 268 days	**Christina Baas-Kaiser** Netherlands Speed Skating	Oldest female gold medalist, individual event (3,000-meter race, 1972)
35 years, 4 days	**Magnar Solberg** Norway Biathlon	Oldest gold medalist, individual event, (men's 20-kilometer race, 1972)
39 years, 353 days	**Raisa Smetanina** Unified Team Cross Country Skiing	Oldest female gold medalist ever (4 x 5-kilometer relay, 1992)
48 years, 357 days	**Jay O'Brien** U.S. Bobsled	Oldest gold medalist ever (four-man bobsled, 1932)

IN NAGANO, TARA LIPINSKI GLIDES ACROSS THE ICE IN THE FREE SKATE PROGRAM THAT CLINCHED THE GOLD MEDAL.

JAY O'BRIEN, FAR RIGHT, AND HIS TEAMMATES POSE WITH THEIR BOBSLED BEFORE WINNING THE GOLD MEDAL IN 1932.

OLYMPIC SNAPSHOTS

EACH EDITION OF THE WINTER GAMES HAS ITS OWN STORIES OF ARTISTRY AND DARING, INNOVATION AND DRAMA. HERE ARE SOME OF THE BREAKTHROUGHS AND HIGHLIGHTS SINCE WINTER SPORTS MADE THEIR DEBUT AT THE OLYMPICS.

BESIDES EARNING A GOLD MEDAL IN WOMEN'S FIGURE SKATING IN 1908, MADGE SYERS, LEFT, TEAMED WITH HER HUSBAND EDGAR TO TAKE THE BRONZE MEDAL IN THE PAIRS.

1908 AND 1920
Winter Sports at the Summer Games

When officials met to draw up the roster of sports for the first modern Olympic Games in 1896, figure skating was listed alongside all the warm-weather activities. Unfortunately there wasn't an ice rink in the host city of Athens, Greece, so plans to hold skating events were canceled. But three figure skating contests did take place at the 1908 Summer Games in London. Florence "Madge" Syers of Great Britain took the gold in the women's event, Sweden's Ulrich Salchow won the men's, and Germans Anna Hübler and Heinrich Burger won the pairs. A year before, Salchow had invented the backwards jump that still bears his name.

No winter sports were contested in 1912, but figure skating was back at the 1920 Summer Olympics in Antwerp, Belgium, and ice hockey was on the roster for the first time. Swedish skaters Gillis Grafström and Magda Julin-Mauroy won the men's and women's singles titles in skating, while a couple from Finland earned the gold in pairs. Canada beat out the U.S. for the gold medal in ice hockey.

1924
1st Winter Games
JANUARY 25 TO FEBRUARY 5
CHAMONIX, FRANCE

Officially, the 258 athletes who went to Chamonix, France, in 1924 competed in an International Winter Sports Week sponsored by the IOC. It wasn't until more than a year later that the IOC decided to hold a Winter Olympiad every four years and to rename the 1924 gathering the First Olympic Winter Games.

Athletes from the snowy Scandinavian countries took 28 of the 43 medals at Chamonix, but the first gold medal went to speed skater Charles Jewtraw, an

American. Fellow speed skater A. Clas Thunberg of Finland won medals in all five races he entered, finishing the Games with three gold medals, one silver, and one bronze. Thorleif Haug of Norway earned gold medals in two cross country skiing events and the Nordic combined. Both the Canadian ice hockey team and Swedish figure skater Gillis Grafström built on their 1920 victories by winning again. Chamonix also saw the first appearance of figure skater Sonja Henie, who would go on to win gold medals at three consecutive Winter Olympiads. Here, however, the 11-year-old Norwegian finished last.

1928
2nd Winter Games
FEBRUARY 11 TO FEBRUARY 19
ST. MORITZ, SWITZERLAND

Wild weather wreaked havoc at the 1928 Winter Games, as soaring temperatures and soaking rains caused all kinds of trouble for athletes and organizers. Cross country skiers started the 50-kilometer race with the morning temperature a crisp 0° Fahrenheit, only to see the course turn to mush as it rose to 77° by noon. Per Erik Hedlund of Sweden ended up capturing the gold in just under five hours, more than one hour slower than the winning time in 1924. That same day, only seven of the ten skaters finished their qualifying heats in the 10,000-meter speed skating race before the ice melted and officials postponed the event. Conditions were just as bad the next day and many of the competitors went home. Irving Jaffee of the United States, who had the fastest time, never got a medal because the race was canceled.

Fortunately, temperatures fell again, allowing for a number of outstanding performances. Sonja Henie dazzled spectators on the way to her first gold medal in figure skating, while Gillis Grafström won his third title in the men's event. A. Clas Thunberg won two more gold medals in speed skating, and the U.S. won the five-man bobsled race with a team led by 16-year-old Billy Fiske. U.S. brothers Jennison and John Heaton finished one-two in the skeleton, a new event that would not be run again until 1948.

OFFICIAL POSTER, 1924

OFFICIAL POSTER, 1928

OFFICIAL POSTER, 1932

SPEED SKATER JACK SHEA, LEFT, AND FIGURE SKATER SONJA HENIE ENJOY A SPOT OF TEA IN LAKE PLACID, 1932.

3rd Winter Games
FEBRUARY 4 TO FEBRUARY 15
LAKE PLACID, NEW YORK

Irving Jaffee had some unfinished business from 1928 on the speed skating oval, and he took care of it in Lake Placid by winning gold medals in both the 5,000-meter and 10,000-meter races. But the speed-skating events were plagued by controversy. Local officials dictated that all of the skaters race together in a pack instead of running timed heats with two racers each. This change in rules so angered superstar A. Clas Thunberg that he withdrew from the Games in protest. In the end, skaters from the U.S. and Canada won 10 of the 12 speed skating medals. Lake Placid native Jack Shea, whose son and grandson also would be Winter Olympians, took the gold in the 500- and 1,500-meter races.

Sonja Henie repeated as gold medalist in women's figure skating, but longtime champion Gillis Grafström came in second to Austria's Karl Schäfer in the men's event. Billy Fiske piloted the U.S. four-man bobsled team to victory, giving crew member Eddie Eagan a winter gold medal to match the gold he had won in light-heavyweight boxing at the 1920 Summer Games. The Lake Placid Games also saw the introduction of the two-man bobsled race, won by local brothers J. Hubert and Curtis Stevens. Though women's speed skating would not be added to the medal program until 1960, some races were run as a demonstration sport. British figure skater Mollie Phillips achieved another milestone for female athletes when she became the first woman to carry her country's flag at the opening ceremonies of the Winter Games.

4th Winter Games
FEBRUARY 6 TO FEBRUARY 16
GARMISCH-PARTENKIRCHEN, GERMANY

Before 1936, only Nordic skiing events—ski jumping and cross country—were contested at the Olympic Winter Games. In Germany, the Alpine combined event, which includes one downhill run and two slalom runs, was added to the men's and women's programs. But with this new event came a new controversy. The IOC ruled that ski instructors could not compete because they were professionals, and Swiss and Austrian skiers boycotted in protest. That helped Germany, whose skiers placed first and second in both the men's and women's Alpine combined. Sonja Henie and Karl Schäfer repeated as gold medalists in figure skating, while Germany's Ernst Baier scored a rare double by winning the silver medal in the men's event and the gold in the pairs. Norwegian speed skater Ivar Ballangrud won three gold medals and a silver, while his countryman Birger Ruud won the ski jumping event for the second Olympics in a row and just missed out on a medal in the Alpine combined. In ice hockey, Great Britain finally found a way to unseat the Canadian team, which had won every gold medal ever contested in the sport. Officials from the British Ice Hockey Federation recruited all of the Canadian players they could find who had been born in Britain. The British gold medal team consisted of 12 players, ten of whom had grown up in Canada and still lived there.

OFFICIAL POSTER, 1936

1940
Canceled

IOC officials chose Sapporo, Japan, as the site for the 1940 Olympic Winter Games, but in 1938 the Japanese withdrew because they were at war with China. Oslo, Norway, and St. Moritz, Switzerland, were considered as alternate sites, but continuing conflicts over Alpine skiing could not be resolved. Finally, the IOC decided to return the Games to Garmisch-Partenkirchen, Germany. By late 1939, however, Germany was engaged in a war with Great Britain, France, Poland, and several other nations and the 1940 Games were canceled.

1944
Canceled

Cortina d'Ampezzo, Italy, won the right to stage the 1944 Winter Games over Oslo, Norway, and Montreal, Canada, but the Games were canceled due to World War II.

WINTER OLYMPICS
POSTAGE STAMP ISSUED
BY GERMANY, 1936

1948

5th Winter Games
JANUARY 30 TO FEBRUARY 8
ST. MORITZ, SWITZERLAND

Weather was a factor again when the Winter Games returned to St. Moritz, though the winds and temperature swings weren't quite as severe as in 1928, and no events were canceled. This first staging of the Games in 12 years saw the return of old champions and the debut of new ones. Ski jumping legend Birger Ruud, who had spent part of World War II in a Nazi prison camp, came to St. Moritz as a coach with the Norwegian team. Ruud, 36, decided to enter the jumping competition at the last minute and won a silver medal. American John Heaton, 39, won his second silver medal in the skeleton, 20 years after the first.

Figure skating crowned two new gold medalists: Barbara Ann Scott of Canada won the women's crown and Dick Button of the U.S. won the men's. An expanded Alpine skiing program of three men's and three women's events saw the U.S. earn its first skiing gold medal when Gretchen Fraser won the slalom. Fraser also took the silver in the Alpine combined. France won its first gold medals ever in individual events when daredevil skier Henri Oreiller finished first in both the downhill and the Alpine combined. He also won the bronze in the slalom. Canada was back on top in ice hockey, but the winning team was almost overshadowed by a controversy involving the U.S. Due to a disagreement between the U.S. Olympic Committee and the International Ice Hockey Federation, two separate U.S. hockey teams made the trip to St. Moritz. Only one was allowed to play, and it finished out of medal contention.

1952

6th Winter Games
FEBRUARY 14 TO FEBRUARY 25
OSLO, NORWAY

Because he helped popularize ski jumping and skiing as sports in the 19th century, Norway's Sondre Nordheim is considered the "Father of Modern Skiing." When Oslo got the nod to stage the 1952 Olympics, organizers chose Nordheim's birthplace in Morgedal as the starting point for the first ever

Winter Games torch relay. Ninety-four skiers relayed the flame from the hearth in Nordheim's home to the capital city, a distance of approximately 140 miles (225 kilometers). The arrival of the torch signaled the start of a Winter Olympiad characterized by excellent weather, enthusiastic fans, and great success for athletes from Norway, Finland, and the United States.

Norwegian standouts included speed skater Hjalmar Andersen, who won three gold medals, and Alpine skier Stein Eriksen, who took silver in the slalom and gold in the newest event, the giant slalom. Behind gold medalist Lydia Wideman, Finland's female skiers swept the first cross country event ever held for women, the 10k. Finnish men won five other medals in cross country, as well as one in ski jumping. Nineteen-year-old Andrea Mead Lawrence of the U.S. won gold medals in the slalom and the giant slalom, while Dick Button repeated as gold medalist in men's figure skating after becoming the first athlete to do a triple loop in competition. America's top female figure skating prospect, Tenley Albright, took the silver, finishing just behind Britain's Jeanette Altwegg. The U.S. also finished second in ice hockey as Canada won the gold once again.

OFFICIAL POSTER, 1952

1956
7th Winter Games
JANUARY 26 TO FEBRUARY 5
CORTINA D'AMPEZZO, ITALY

A surprise triple gold medalist, a courageous figure skater, and a new powerhouse national team made their marks at Cortina, as TV cameras captured the action of the Winter Games for the first time. Viewers watched Austria's Anton "Toni" Sailer sweep the giant slalom, slalom, and downhill to become only the fifth Winter Olympian to win three gold medals at a single Games. They saw Tenley Albright of the U.S., who had overcome polio as a child, capture the gold in figure skating despite suffering a serious cut to her right ankle in practice. And they saw athletes from the Soviet Union win 16 medals, including seven gold, in that nation's first appearance at the Winter Games.

Soviet athletes made their presence known in

LEFT TO RIGHT, FIGURE SKATERS RONALD ROBERTSON (SILVER), HAYES ALAN JENKINS (GOLD), AND DAVID JENKINS (BRONZE) ENJOY THE FIRST EVER MEDAL SWEEP BY U.S. ATHLETES IN A WINTER GAMES EVENT, 1956.

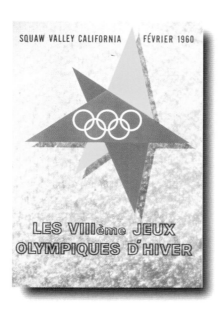

OFFICIAL POSTER, 1960

speed skating and cross country skiing, winning seven medals in each sport. But their gold medal in ice hockey signaled the beginning of a new era. Showing evidence of superior training and discipline, the Soviets won seven games without a defeat, shutting out the defending champion Canadian team in the final, 2–0. After winning six of the first seven gold medals in Olympic ice hockey, Canada would not take the gold again until 2002. Fittingly, the goaltender for the 2002 Canadian team would be Martin Brodeur, whose father, Denis, was one of Canada's goalies in 1956.

1960
8th Winter Games
FEBRUARY 18 TO FEBRUARY 28
SQUAW VALLEY, CALIFORNIA

When Squaw Valley won the chance to host the eighth Winter Games in 1955, the ski resort had little more than a chairlift, a few rope tows, and a 50-room lodge. By 1960 organizers had added a ski jump, an outdoor speed skating oval, an indoor figure skating and hockey arena, and an inn with rooms for 750 athletes. The only item left out was a bobsled run. Since only nine of the 30 nations coming to the Games intended to bring bobsledders, the organizers decided to cut that event from the program. In its place, they added the first medal events ever in women's speed skating, as well as the men's biathlon, a sport that combines cross country skiing and rifle shooting.

Klas Lestander of Sweden won the inaugural biathlon competition, while Soviet women won gold medals in three of the four speed skating events, with Lydia Skoblikova taking the 1,500-meter and 3,000-meter titles. Meanwhile, U.S. athletes won all three of their gold medals at the indoor ice arena. Carol Heiss improved upon her 1956 silver medal in figure skating by taking the gold. In the men's event, David Jenkins won a gold medal to match the one earned in 1956 by his brother, Hayes Alan Jenkins. But the most unexpected U.S. victory came in ice hockey. Behind goalie Jack McCartan and brothers Roger and Billy Christian, the U.S. "Team of Destiny" defeated Canada, the Soviet Union, and Czechoslovakia to take the first ever U.S. gold medal in the sport.

1964
9th Winter Games
JANUARY 29 TO FEBRUARY 9
INNSBRUCK, AUSTRIA

Lydia Skoblikova's performance at Innsbruck remains one of the most impressive in Olympic history. The 24-year-old Soviet school teacher won gold medals in all four of the women's speed skating events in four straight days. She was the first athlete, male or female, to win four individual gold medals at any single Winter or Summer Olympiad. Her victories led the Soviet team as they amassed a total of 25 medals, 11 of them gold.

Beyond the speed skating oval, the Innsbruck Games saw a number of additions and innovations. A second ski jumping event was added to the program, as was the sport of luge, in which men and women on sleds speed feet first down an icy course. For the first time, computer use was widespread and Alpine skiing times were measured in hundredths of a second. Among the most noteworthy Alpine events were the slalom and giant slalom, where French sisters Christine and Marielle Goitschel battled each other. Christine won the gold and Marielle the silver in the slalom, while the standings were reversed in the giant slalom. In cross country skiing, Sweden's Sixten Jernberg won two gold medals and a bronze, ending his career with four gold, three silver, and two bronze medals over three Olympiads. The Soviet Union won the gold in ice hockey and also began its long winning streak in the figure skating pairs contest. And three years after the top U.S. figure skaters and coaches died in a tragic plane crash, Scott Allen won the country's only medal in the sport, a bronze.

1968
10th Winter Games
FEBRUARY 6 TO FEBRUARY 18
GRENOBLE, FRANCE

Controversies abounded when the Winter Games returned to France for the first time since 1924, but there were many excellent performances as well. And they were seen by audiences around the world as these were the first Winter Games to be broadcast live and in color via satellite. Peggy Fleming captivated fans with

OFFICIAL POSTER, 1964

WITH NINE MEDALS COLLECTED OVER THREE OLYMPIADS, SIXTEN JERNBERG, SHOWN HERE IN 1964, REMAINS ONE OF THE LEADING WINTER OLYMPIC MEDAL WINNERS OF ALL TIME.

OFFICIAL POSTER, 1968

GOALTENDER VLADISLAV TRETIAK
WOULD LEAD THE SOVIET UNION
TO ICE HOCKEY GOLD MEDALS IN
1972, 1976, AND 1984.

her elegance and strength to take the women's figure skating crown and earn the only gold medal won by the U.S. Eugenio Monti of Italy won both the two-man and four-man bobsled events after earning two silver medals in 1956 and two bronze medals in 1964. Canadian skier Nancy Greene won the giant slalom and took the silver medal in the slalom. Franco Nones of Italy won the 30-kilometer cross country race and became the first non-Scandinavian man to win an individual event in cross country.

Local hero Jean-Claude Killy's three gold medals in Alpine skiing thrilled the French crowd, though a protest by Austria's Karl Schranz almost took the slalom medal away from him. Schranz claimed that a man had crossed in front of him as he was taking his second slalom run on the foggy course, causing him to miss a gate. The referee allowed Schranz to repeat the run, and his new time thrust him into the gold medal position. But a review of the tape showed that Schranz had missed two gates before he claimed to have seen the intruder, and he was disqualified. Elsewhere, the first, second, and fourth finishers in the women's luge competition, all East Germans, were disqualified for heating the runners on their sleds to make them slide faster. And the IOC instituted drug testing for all athletes and gender testing for women. The gender tests, meant to stop men from disguising themselves to compete in women's events, would be discontinued before the 2002 Games.

1972
11th Winter Games
FEBRUARY 3 TO FEBRUARY 13
SAPPORO, JAPAN

Conflicts over the IOC's rules on amateurism came to a head in 1972 as the Winter Games were staged in Asia for the first time. Avery Brundage, president of the IOC, threatened to ban ten Alpine skiers for taking payments from the manufacturers of skiing equipment. Instead, he banned the one athlete he considered the worst offender, Austria's Karl Schranz. Meanwhile, the Canadian ice hockey team boycotted the Games to protest what they saw as a double standard in determining who was eligible for the Olympics. IOC rules banned professional hockey players, but allowed full-time players from Communist countries because they were considered "government employees" rather than pro athletes. Despite these tensions, spectators witnessed many notable athletic achievements, including those by Japan's ski jumpers. Before 1972, Japan had won only one medal at any Winter Games, a silver in the slalom in 1956. But Japan's ski jumpers drew enormous cheers as they swept the medals on the normal hill (70-meter jump), with Yukio Kasaya taking the gold. Elsewhere, Francisco Fernández Ochoa won the gold in the slalom, Spain's first Winter Games medal ever. Switzerland's Marie-Thérèse Nadig won the women's downhill and giant slalom, while speed skater Adrianus "Ard" Schenk of the Netherlands earned gold medals in the 1,500-meter, 5,000-meter, and 10,000-meter races. U.S. men managed only one medal, a silver in ice hockey, while the women took home seven medals in all. Speed skaters Dianne Holum and Anne Henning and Alpine skier Barbara Cochran all won gold medals for the U.S.

1976
12th Winter Games
FEBRUARY 4 TO FEBRUARY 15
INNSBRUCK, AUSTRIA

Denver, Colorado, won the bid to host the 12th Winter Games, but had to withdraw in late 1972 after its citizens voted to stop the local Olympic committee from using public funds for the venture. The people of Denver were worried about the impact of the Games on the environment, as well as the great expense of building new roads and arenas. With just over three years until the opening ceremonies, the IOC turned to Innsbruck, which could use many of the structures from the 1964 Games. In welcoming back the Olympics, Austrians also welcomed the chance to reverse their fortunes in skiing. It fell on the shoulders of downhill racer Franz Klammer to erase the bitterness many of his countrymen had felt since the IOC banned Karl Schranz in 1972. Klammer won the gold, skiing wildly at an average speed of 63.9 miles (102.8 kilometers) per hour in what was then the

AUSTRIA'S FRANZ KLAMMER SKIS TO VICTORY IN THE MEN'S DOWNHILL AT THE 1976 WINTER GAMES.

BEFORE THE 1976 OLYMPICS
WERE MOVED TO INNSBRUCK,
A FEW SOUVENIRS, SUCH AS THIS
PIN, WERE ISSUED COMMEMO-
RATING THE DENVER GAMES.

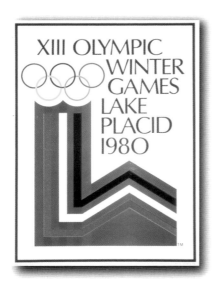

OFFICIAL POSTER, 1980

fastest downhill run in Olympic history.

On the women's side, Rosi Mittermaier of West Germany won the downhill and the slalom and came within twelve hundredths of a second of winning the giant slalom as well. Americans Peter Mueller and Sheila Young both won gold medals in speed skating, with Young earning silver and bronze medals, too. Bill Koch became the first and only U.S. athlete ever to medal in cross country when he won the silver in the 30-kilometer race. Ice dancing was introduced as the newest event in figure skating, with the Soviet couple of Lyudmila Pakhomova and Aleksandr Gorshkov winning the gold. In the individual figure skating events, John Curry of Great Britain won the men's title with an elegant, balletic program, while Dorothy Hamill of the U.S. won the women's with athletic jumps and spins. In ice hockey, Sweden joined Canada's ongoing boycott of the competition, leaving the Soviet Union to take the gold.

1980
13th Winter Games
FEBRUARY 13 TO FEBRUARY 24
LAKE PLACID, NEW YORK

Forty-eight years had passed since the first Lake Placid Olympics, and the Winter Games had grown so much that the small New York village now had difficulty containing them. Despite overcrowding, traffic jams, and bad weather, however, the Games gave a number of athletes a chance to excel. Foremost among them was U.S. speed skater Eric Heiden, who dominated his sport as no one had before. Heiden won all five events on the men's speed skating program, setting an Olympic record in each race and a world record in the 10,000. He remains the only athlete ever to win five gold medals at a single Winter Games.

In Alpine skiing, Ingemar Stenmark of Sweden won the men's slalom and giant slalom while Hanni Wenzel of Lichtenstein won both events on the women's side and also took the silver medal in the downhill. Irina Rodnina of the Soviet Union achieved an impressive milestone when she won the pairs competition with her husband Aleksandr Zaitsev. It was Rodnina's third gold medal in a row in the pairs, with two different partners. Ulrich Wehling of East Germany scored a three-peat as well, in the Nordic Combined. But once again, the ice hockey arena was the site of the most unlikely victory. There the U.S. hockey team, made up mostly of college students, met the formidable Soviet Union squad in the medal round and managed to beat them, 4–3. This "Miracle on Ice" so captivated the host nation that even Eric Heiden called it the greatest moment of the 1980 Winter Games. Two days later, the U.S. team beat Finland in the final, 4–2, to capture the gold medal.

1984
14th Winter Games
FEBRUARY 8 TO FEBRUARY 19
SARAJEVO, YUGOSLAVIA

Athletes from the U.S. broke through in a big way in Sarajevo, especially in the skiing events. Bill Johnson became the first American man ever to win the downhill, with a record-breaking average speed of 64.9 miles (104.5 kilometers) per hour. Twin brothers Phil and Steve Mahre finished first and second, respectively, in the slalom, while Debbie Armstrong took the gold and Christin Cooper the silver in the women's giant slalom. In figure skating, Scott Hamilton won the gold in the men's event, while Rosalynn Sumners finished second to East Germany's Katarina Witt in the women's. And brother-and-sister pairs skaters Kitty and Peter Carruthers performed a terrific free skate routine to take the silver medal behind the Soviet Union's Yelena Valova and Oleg Vasilyev.

Elsewhere, in her third Winter Olympics, Finland's Marja-Lissa Hämäläinen won gold medals in all three of the women's individual cross country events and a bronze in the relay. East Germany won both bobsled contests, but Swedish bobsledder Carl-Erik Eriksson earned the distinction of competing in his sixth Winter Games. Soviet goalie Vladislav Tretiak led his team to gold for the third time. Ice dancing reached a new level of brilliance when Great Britain's Jayne Torvill and Christopher Dean tallied perfect 6.0 scores in artistic interpretation from every judge on the way to the gold medal. And Jure Franko

OFFICIAL POSTER, 1984

PHIL MAHRE OF THE U.S. ATTACKS THE SLALOM COURSE ON THE WAY TO A GOLD MEDAL, 1984.

brought delight to the host country by winning Yugoslavia's first Winter Olympics medal ever, a silver in the giant slalom. Only eight years after these Games, his country would be torn apart by a brutal war that would leave Sarajevo in a shambles.

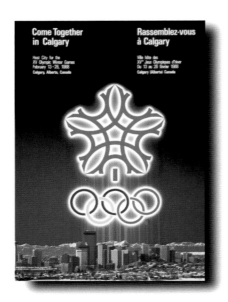

OFFICIAL POSTER, 1988

1988
15th Winter Games
FEBRUARY 13 TO FEBRUARY 28
CALGARY, CANADA

From 1984 through 2002, the IOC would double the number of events at the Winter Games, and in Calgary it took the first step by adding seven contests. New in Alpine skiing were the men's and women's super giant slalom ("super G") and the return of the Alpine combined. The other additions were team contests in ski jumping and the Nordic combined and a 5,000-meter speed skating race for women. Yvonne van Gennip of the Netherlands won the 5,000 in world record time and also earned gold medals in the 1,500-meter and 3,000-meter races. Elsewhere in women's speed skating, Bonnie Blair of the U.S. took the gold in the 500 meters and the bronze in the 1,000 meters.

Other outstanding performers in Calgary included ski jumper Matti Nykänen of Finland, who won three gold medals, including one in the team event. Alberto Tomba of Italy won the slalom and giant slalom Alpine races on the men's side, while Vreni Schneider of Switzerland won both races on the women's side. Katarina Witt repeated as the women's gold medalist in figure skating, while Brian Boitano of the U.S. narrowly beat out Brian Orser of Canada for the men's title. The Soviet Union won its seventh gold medal in ice hockey, while Finland took the silver, its first hockey medal ever. And the 1988 Winter Games saw the participation of black athletes in a variety of sports for the first time. U.S. figure skater Debi Thomas, Alpine skier Seba Johnson of the Virgin Islands, and several bobsledders, including the storied Jamaican bobsled team, helped bring to the Winter Games more of the diversity that the Summer Olympics had long enjoyed.

ALTHOUGH THE JAMAICAN BOBSLED TEAM FINISHED LAST IN THEIR FIRST WINTER GAMES IN 1988, THEY IMPROVED TO 14TH IN 1994, BEATING BOTH SQUADS FROM THE U.S. THE TEAM WAS IMMORTALIZED IN THE 1993 FILM *COOL RUNNINGS*.

1992

16th Winter Games
FEBRUARY 8 TO FEBRUARY 23
ALBERTVILLE, FRANCE

Expansion continued at the Winter Games in Albertville, as freestyle skiing and short track speed skating were added to the program, along with three events in women's biathlon. Donna Weinbrecht of the U.S. won the gold medal in the inaugural women's freestyle event, the moguls, while Edgar Grospiron of France took the men's gold. Korea's Kim Ki-hoon won the men's 1,000-meter short track event and led his team to victory in the 5,000-meter relay. On the women's side, Cathy Turner of the U.S. won the 500-meter short track race and helped the U.S. relay team earn a silver medal behind Canada.

Kristi Yamaguchi of the U.S. took the gold in women's figure skating, while Viktor Petrenko of the Unified Team (formerly the Soviet Union) beat out Paul Wylie of the U.S. on the men's side. Bonnie Blair repeated as winner of the 500-meter speed skating race and won the 1,000 meters as well. And the 1992 Winter Games saw records set at both ends of the age spectrum. Toni Nieminen led Finland to the gold in the team ski jumping event and became the youngest male gold medalist ever. Raisa Smetanina won the cross country relay with the Unified Team and became the oldest female gold medalist ever. It was Smetanina's fourth gold medal and her tenth medal overall. She was the first woman to win medals at five Winter Games in a row.

1994

17th Winter Games
FEBRUARY 12 TO FEBRUARY 27
LILLEHAMMER, NORWAY

Coming just two years after Albertville, the Lillehammer Games helped to establish a new schedule for the Winter Olympics, which would now take place two years before each Summer Olympiad, in 1994, 1998, 2002, and so on. The short time span between the Albertville and Lillehammer Games gave athletes a unique opportunity to extend their dominance. Speed skater Bonnie Blair added two more gold medals to her total and became the first woman

OFFICIAL POSTER, 1992

TICKETS TO AN OLYMPIC ICE HOCKEY MATCH, 1994

to win the 500-meter race three times in a row. Alberto Tomba won a silver medal in the slalom to bring his medal total to five, won over three Olympiads. Cross country skier Lyubov Yegorova of Russia, who had won three gold and two silver medals in Albertville, added three more gold medals and one more silver. And Norwegian speed skater Johann Olav Koss, already the winner of a gold and a silver in 1992, won three gold medals in Lillehammer and set three world records in the process.

Other standouts included Manuela Di Centa of Italy, who won a medal in each of the five women's cross country races. Kim Yoon-mi of Korea won a gold medal in the short track speed skating relay and became the youngest medalist at any Winter Games. Alpine skier Tommy Moe won the downhill and earned a silver in the super G for the best performance by a U.S. male skier to date. And Oksana Baiul of Ukraine won a women's figure skating contest that was overshadowed by the bizarre drama involving U.S. skaters Tonya Harding and Nancy Kerrigan. Harding, whose former husband had hired men to injure Kerrigan in a failed attempt to keep her out of the Games, finished eighth. Kerrigan took the silver.

1998
18th Winter Games
FEBRUARY 7 TO FEBRUARY 22
NAGANO, JAPAN

Among the most memorable images of the 1998 Winter Games are a spectacular crash and a ski jumper soaring through a blizzard to the cheers of 40,000 ecstatic fans. The crash, on the Alpine downhill course, saw Austria's Hermann Maier awkwardly take flight, plunge onto his head, somersault through two safety nets, and finally land in a pile of snow. Miraculously, Maier wasn't seriously injured. Even more remarkably, he returned three days later to take the gold medal in the super G and three days after that to win the giant slalom. Ski jumper Masahiko Harada's efforts also ended in triumph. In front of his home crowd, Harada tied the Olympic large-hill distance record with his second jump and helped bring his team the gold.

CATHY TURNER OF THE U.S. LEADS ZHANG YANMEI OF CHINA IN THE WOMEN'S 500-METER SHORT TRACK SPEED SKATING RACE, 1994. TURNER WOULD WIN THE GOLD AND ZHANG THE SILVER DESPITE A CHINESE PROTEST THAT THE AMERICAN HAD USED ILLEGAL TACTICS TO GET AHEAD.

Nagano saw the return of curling to the Olympics after 74 years, as well as the introduction of men's and women's snowboarding and women's ice hockey. The U.S. women's hockey team won the gold medal, while the men's gold went to the Czech Republic. Speed skating records fell in every event as athletes used the new clap skates, made with hinges that kept the blade on the ice longer as a skater began to lift his or her foot. Tara Lipinski of the U.S. won the women's figure skating gold and replaced Sonja Henie as the youngest winner of an individual event at the Winter Games. Katja Seizinger of Germany became the first skier to win gold medals in the downhill twice and also took the gold in the Alpine combined and the bronze in the giant slalom. And in cross country skiing, Bjørn Dæhlie of Norway won three gold medals and one silver for a career total of eight gold medals and four silvers over three Olympiads. He remains the leading medal winner in the history of the Winter Games.

OFFICIAL POSTER, 1998

2002
19th Winter Games
FEBRUARY 8 TO FEBRUARY 24
SALT LAKE CITY, UTAH

While the 19th Winter Games were the scene of many record-breaking performances and an unprecedented 34 medals for U.S. athletes, they also had their share of scandal and controversy. The problems started in November 1998, when evidence surfaced that IOC members had accepted bribes in exchange for voting to grant the Games to Salt Lake City. The ensuing investigations led to the firing or resignation of 19 members of the IOC and several officials from the Salt Lake Organizing Committee. There was other trouble during the Games. Seven cross country skiers failed drug tests, including three gold medalists who were stripped of their medals. And a major controversy erupted when Canadian pairs skaters Jamie Salé and David Pelletier performed a near-perfect program, only to see the gold medal go to their Russian opponents. After one of the judges for the event admitted she had been pressured to vote for the Russians, the IOC quickly awarded the Canadians a second pair of gold medals.

IN 2002, CANADIAN GOALIE MARTIN BRODEUR HONORS HIS FATHER DENIS, THE GOALIE FOR CANADA AT THE 1956 WINTER GAMES.

OFFICIAL ICE HOCKEY PUCK, 2002

On a positive note, the Games came off without incident, despite fears in the wake of the terrorist attacks of September 11, 2001. Sarah Hughes gave the U.S. crowd something to cheer about when she earned the gold medal in women's figure skating. American Jim Shea honored the memory of his grandfather, 1932 double gold-medalist Jack Shea, by winning the gold in the skeleton. Canada won its first gold medal in men's ice hockey in 50 years, taking the title in women's ice hockey as well. Vonetta Flowers of the U.S. became the first black athlete to earn a gold medal at the Winter Games when she and Jill Bakken won the inaugural women's bobsled event. Janica Kostelic of Croatia collected three gold medals and a silver and became the first Alpine skier to win four medals at a single Games. And Kjetil André Aamodt of Norway won the super G and the Alpine combined to bring his total medal count over four Winter Games to seven, the most ever for an Alpine skier.

2006
20th Winter Games
FEBRUARY 10 TO FEBRUARY 26
TORINO, ITALY

With some 2,200,000 people in the city and its surroundings, Turin (Torino in Italian) will be the largest metropolitan area ever to host the Winter Games. The opening and closing ceremonies and most indoor events will take place in Turin, while the curling competition will be in Pinerolo, about 22 miles (36 kilometers) to the southwest. All of the other events will be contested at various sites in the Italian Alps, from 53 miles (85 kilometers) to 62 miles (100 kilometers) away.

NEVE   GLIZ

2006 OLYMPIC MASCOTS NEVE
(REPRESENTING A SNOWBALL) AND
GLIZ (A BLOCK OF ICE)

2010
21st Winter Games
FEBRUARY 12 TO FEBRUARY 28
VANCOUVER, CANADA

Plans call for the ice events to take place in Vancouver itself, while most of the snow events will be held 78 miles (125 kilometers) away, in Whistler. Each location will have its own athletes' village.

In Salt Lake City, a banner of a speed skater overlooks the flags of many nations displayed in the plaza where athletes received their medals at the 2002 Winter Games.

SOURCES AND QUOTES

IT'S HARD TO IMAGINE that a summertime lunch at a Pizzeria Uno restaurant in New Jersey would help inspire me to write a book on the Winter Olympics, but that's exactly what happened. It didn't hurt that my luncheon companion was Donna Weinbrecht, a three-time Olympian and the first-ever female gold medalist in mogul skiing. Over Caesar salad and thin-crust pizza, this freestyle pioneer shared her memories of winning, coming back from injuries, and dealing with the ever-changing conditions of Olympic ski courses. Her descriptions were so evocative that I half expected snowplows to be clearing the streets when I exited the restaurant.

Soon after Weinbrecht helped me wrap my head around the dynamics of winter sports, I headed to the library at the Amateur Athletic Foundation of Los Angeles (AAFLA) to gather everything I could on the history and evolution of the Olympic Winter Games. This library, called the Paul Ziffren Sports Resource Center, yielded much terrific material when I visited it while working on *Swifter, Higher, Stronger*, my book on the Summer Olympics. And my return visit was just as successful. Over the course of several days, I pored over books, magazines, journals, and newspapers and collected articles, oral histories, statistics, and bibliographies that helped me begin to formulate the story of the Winter Games. When I returned home I supplemented this research by accessing the AAFLA Web site, *www.aafla.org*, which includes a digital archive of more than 40,000 documents focusing on Olympic and sports history. I also scoured *The Complete Book of the Winter Olympics* by David Wallechinsky, an essential resource of statistics and anecdotes that had a permanent place on my desk the entire time I was working on this book. Other important references, including David Miller's *Athens to Athens: The Official History of the Olympic Games and the IOC, 1894–2004* and *Frozen in Time: The Greatest Moments at the Winter Olympics* by Bud Greenspan, are noted with brief descriptions on the following page.

As with my last book, most of the photo research for Freeze Frame was undertaken online using the search technology on the sites of photo agencies in the United States and Europe. Once again the process of looking for photographs added another dimension to my research as I came face-to-face with yesterday's heroes. Seeing the 1956 torchbearer sprawled out on the ice after he tripped over television cables (see page 80) spoke volumes about the awkward introduction of television at the Winter Games. Finding a 1961 photo of a charred copy of Sports Illustrated in the wreckage of the plane crash in which cover athlete Laurence Owen died (see page 34) brought home the enormity of that tragedy. Each photograph in this book tells a story of its own, and the new accessibility of online photo research tools made it possible to sift through tens of thousands of shots to find the ones that worked best with the text.

Finally, in the interest of accountability, the sources of all the quotations used in this book are included below. Full citations are given the first time a source is mentioned. After that, with a few exceptions, only the title and page number are noted. Books and Web sites of special interest to young readers or their parents or teachers are listed, with commentary, on the Resources page.

CHAPTER 1: This Snowy Prelude
p. 14, Coubertin ("Pre-Olympic Winter Games," by Yves Morales, *Encyclopedia of the Modern Olympic Movement*, p. 272); p. 15, "the father of Swedish sport" ("Skating and Olympism," *Olympic Review*, May 1984, p. 354); p. 15, Balck ("The Nordic Games and the Origins of the Olympic Winter Games," by Ron Edgeworth, *Citius, Altius, Fortius*, November 1994, p. 29); p. 15, Salchow (*The 1908 Olympic Games: Results for All Competitors in All Events, with Commentary* by Bill Mallon and Ian Buchanan, Jefferson, McFarland, 2000, p. 15); p. 16, "Ragtag immigrant kids" ("Immigration and Multiculturalism: Introduction," Laurier Institution, 2003, *http://www.education2010.ca/culture/prog_culturaldiversity/indexprint.htm*); p. 16, "This snowy prelude" (*Olympic Memoirs* by Pierre de Coubertin, reprinted in *Olympic Review*, July 1978, p. 434); p. 18, "only it seemed out of courtesy..." ("Americans in the Winter Olympics," *Literary Digest*, February 16, 1924, p. 64); p. 18, Thunberg (*Athens to Athens: The Official History of the Olympic Games and the IOC, 1894-2004* by David Miller, Edinburgh: Mainstream Publishing, 2003, p. 76); p. 19, descriptions of Loughran and Planck-Szabó ("Americans in the Winter Olympics," p. 64); p. 19, Planck-Szabó (*Athens to Athens*, p. 76); p. 19, Coubertin (Pierre de Coubertin, "Speech at the Closing Ceremony of the Winter Games, Chamonix, February 5, 1924" in *Olympism: Selected Writings* by Pierre de Coubertin, Lausanne, Switzerland: IOC, 2000, p. 524).

CHAPTER 2: The Inescapable Weather Jinx p. 21, "The weather gods..." ("Sports of the Times: The Refrigerated Whammy," by Arthur Daley, *New York Times*, January 26, 1964); p. 22, "The thaw..." (*Olympic Memoirs* by Pierre de Coubertin, reprinted in *Olympic Review*, July 1978, p. 434); p. 26, Donna Weinbrecht (*Superwomen: 100 Women, 100 Sports* by Jodi Buren, New York: Bullfinch Press, 2004); p. 27, Picabo Street ("1998 Nagano Olympics: Golden Skates," *CNN/SI*, February 10, 1998, *http://sportsillustrated.cnn.com/olympics/events/1998/nagano/news/1998/02/10/roundup/*); p. 27, "Piped into warm living rooms" ("Sports of the Times: Life in the Chilblain Set," by Arthur Daley, *New York Times*, February 14, 1960); p. 27, Caption ("1998 Nagano Olympics: Sayonara Nagano," *CNN/SI*, February 22, 1998, *http://sportsillustrated.cnn.com/olympics/events/1998/nagano/news/1998/02/22/roundup/*).

CHAPTER 3: Heroes and Superstars
p. 29, Eugenio Monti (*Athens to Athens*, p. 165); p. 31, on Toni Sailer ("Austrians Take Downhill Skiing and Pair Figure-Skating Titles," by Fred Tupper, *New York Times*, February 4, 1956, p. 14); p. 34, "Maybe if things had stayed..." (*The Complete Book of the Winter Olympics* by David Wallechinsky, Woodstock: The Overlook Press, 2001, p. 122); p. 34, "That's simple..." (*Frozen in Time: The Greatest Moments at the Winter Olympics* by Bud Greenspan, Los Angeles: General Publishing Group, 1997, p. 23); p. 35, "capped one of the finest showings" ("Czechoslovak Six Drops 9-4 Contest," by Michael Strauss, *New York Times*, February 29, 1980, p. 34); p. 39, "the most beautiful and emotional moment" (*Frozen in Time*, p. 99); p. 41, "In Norwegian eyes" ("Dæhlie: Winner Who Took It All," BBC Sport Web site, January 14, 2002, *http://news.bbc.co.uk/winterolympics2002/hi/english/other_skiing/newsid_1595000/1595283.stm*).

CHAPTER 4: Intimate Conflicts
p. 47, "Harding blew her medal hopes..." (*The Complete Book of the Winter Olympics*, p. 69); p. 50, "The Olympic Games are...amateur" ("Mr. Avery Brundage's Reply to Dr. Willy Meisl's Article," *Olympic Review*, 1957, pp. 55-56); p. 50, "We have heard much" ("Ski-Brand Controversy Taken Off Table and Swept Under Rug," by Lloyd Garrison, *New York Times*, February 8, 1968); p. 51, "a poisonous tumor" ("Skiing and the Olympic Games," by Sigge Bergman, *Olympic Review*, April 1980, p. 169); p. 51, "If Mr. Brundage had been poor" (*Athens to Athens*, p. 189); p. 51, "A serious mistake" ("Skiing and the Olympic Games," p. 169); p. 57, "unavoidably prejudiced" ("Selling American Civilization: The Olympic Games of 1920 and American Culture" by Mark Dyreson, *Olympika: The International Journal of Olympic Studies*, 1999); p. 57, "for the most part" (*Farewell to Sport* by Paul Gallico, New York: Knopf, 1938, pp. 331-333, quoted in "Return to the Melting Pot: Reviving an Old American Olympic Story," by Mark Dyreson, *The Global Nexus Engaged: Past, Present, Future Interdisciplinary Olympic Studies*, October, 2002, p. 105-112).

CHAPTER 5: Going to Extremes
p. 60, National Sporting Goods Association Statistics ("Snowboarding Blazes New Trails," by Barbara Lloyd, *New York Times*, December 14, 1995, p. B21); p. 61, "sheer unadulterated athletic lunacy" ("The Media Business: Advertising," by Stuart Elliott, *New York Times*, June 21, 1996); p. 64, Michelle Taggart and Ross Powers ("The XVIII Winter Games: Snowboarding," by Ira Berkow, *New York Times*, February 7, 1998); p. 64, "Snowboarding is about fresh tracks" (*The Complete Book of the Winter Olympics*, p. 341); p. 65, "to make sure we have sports" ("Snowboarding Adds New Feel to Olympics," *ESPN.com*, February 25, 2002, *http://sports.espn.go.com/winter02/snowboard/news?id=1340599*); p. 65, "The Commission noted..." ("Review of the Olympic Programme and the Recommendations on the Programme of the XX Olympic Winter Games, Turin 2006," Olympic Programme Commission Executive Board Report, August 2002); p. 65, caption ("Snowboard Cross Is Fast, Scary and Still Not Ready for Winter Olympics," Canadian Press, December 7, 2001, *http://www.active.com/story.cfm?story_id=8335*); p. 66, "just about the burliest comp..." ("Identity Crisis," by B. J. Smith, *EXPN.com*, January 29, 2005); p. 66, Chris Klug and Mark Schulz ("Winter X Games Cherishes High-Risk Atmosphere," by Meri-Jo Borzilleri, KRT Wire, January 29, 2005, *http://www.mercurynews.com/mld/mercurynews/sports/10768539.htm?1c*); p. 66, Eric Heiden ("Olympics Notebook," *St. Petersburg Times*, February 20, 2002); p. 67, Tricia Stumpf, Jim Shea, and Tricia Byrnes ("Winter Athletes Defying Danger," by Paula Parrish, *Cincinnati Post*, February 8, 2002); p. 67, Birger Ruud (*Athens to Athens*, p. 108).

RESOURCES

BOOKS

Brennan, Christine. *Inside Edge: A Revealing Journey into the Secret World of Figure Skating.* New York: Scribner, 1996.

Published in the aftermath of the Tonya Harding–Nancy Kerrigan affair, this is a fascinating, behind-the-scenes look at the skaters, coaches, and judges on the figure skating circuit by one of the most insightful sportswriters working today.

Fleming, Peggy, with Peter Kaminsky. *The Long Program: Skating toward Life's Victories.* New York: Pocket Books, 1999.

With characteristic grace, Fleming recounts her life as an athlete, TV analyst, wife, and mother and discusses how the strength she developed as a skater helped her later in life in her battle against breast cancer.

Greenspan, Bud. *Frozen in Time: The Greatest Moments at the Winter Olympics.* Los Angeles: General Publishing Group, 1997.

In this book, the renowned Olympic filmmaker and historian offers compelling profiles and dynamic photographs of many of the pivotal athletes and teams from the Winter Games.

Kwan, Michelle. *Heart of a Champion: An Autobiography.* New York: Scholastic, 1997.

Written with impressive clarity and self-awareness when Kwan was just 17 years old, this book gives young people an inside look at the joys and pressures of the world of elite figure skating.

Miller, David. *Athens to Athens: The Official History of the Olympic Games and the IOC, 1894–2004.* Edinburgh: Mainstream Publishing, 2003.

This thorough British reference book combines readable accounts of each Winter and Summer Olympics with an ongoing history of the International Olympic Committee. Most outstanding are the introductions to the chapters on the Olympiads, which feature reflections by a diverse lineup of athletes of their own moments in the sun.

Wallechinsky, David. *The Complete Book of the Winter Olympics.* Woodstock: Overlook Press, 2001.

A companion to Wallechinsky's book on the Summer Olympics, this volume is packed with facts and figures on the Winter Games. Wallechinsky gives the final results of every event in every sport and includes hundreds of anecdotes and little-known facts about the athletes involved. He publishes an updated edition in each Olympic year.

WEB SITES

Amateur Athletic Foundation of Los Angeles
www.aafla.org

Fast becoming the best online resource for archival sports material, the digital archive on this site now features the Official Report from each edition of the Winter and Summer Olympics through 2002. There are also PDF files of sports magazines and journals dating back to the 19th century, all easily searchable online. Beyond the archive, this site offers Olympic curriculum guides tied to a number of subject areas, oral histories, a Web arcade of Olympic games, and more.

International Olympic Committee
www.olympic.org

Not only does this "official Web site of the Olympic movement" feature excellent summaries of each edition of the Winter and Summer Games, it also contains free one- to three-minute video highlights of many memorable performances, from Billy Fiske's bobsled victory in 1932 to the majesty of Torvill and Dean in 1984 to Hermann Maier's horrifying crash in 1998. Plus, there are scores of athlete profiles, detailed descriptions of every Olympic sport, and virtual exhibits from the Olympic Museum in Lausanne, Switzerland.

Torino 2006 and Vancouver 2010
www.torino.org and www.vancouver2010.com

These official Web sites of the 2006 and 2010 Winter Games will chronicle preparations for the Games, as well as highlighting results and outstanding performances once the Games take place. Each one also offers educational resources and links to other valuable Olympic sites on the Web.

PLACES TO VISIT

Lake Placid Winter Olympic Museum
Lake Placid, New York
518-523-1655

Relive the highlights of the 1932 and 1980 Olympic Winter Games at this museum in the heart of Lake Placid through oral histories, photos, videos, and exhibits of memorabilia.

Utah Snowboard Museum
Salt Lake City, Utah
801-467-8000, www.saltypeaks.com

Dennis Nazari, owner of the Salty Peaks Snowboard Shop, has amassed what he purports is the largest collection of snowboards anywhere in the world. Among the 620 or so snowboards are several Snurfers, as well as other models from the sport's colorful history.

INDEX

PICTURE CREDITS

Abbreviations: t–top, b–bottom, c–center, l–left, and r–right

Front cover © Steve Griffin/The Salt Lake Tribune/Corbis; Back cover (t) Shaun Botterill/Allsport/Getty Images; (c) Central Press/Getty Images; (b) Trudy Fisher; (background) Clive Brunskill/Getty Images; Quiz, AP/Wide World Photos/Rick Bowmer; pages 2-3 AP/Wide World Photos/John Gaps III; 5 IOC Olympic Museum/Allsport/Getty Images; 6 Staff/AFP/Getty Images; 7 Harry Langdon; 8 AP/Wide World Photos/Tom Hanson; 9 Timothy A. Clary/AFP/Getty Images; 10 (tl) Central Press/Getty Images; (c) Tim De Waele/Isosport/Corbis; (bl) Cris Bouroncle/AFP/Getty Images; (tr) Jerome Delay/ AFP/Getty Images; (br) Donald Miralle/Getty Images; 11 (tl) Roberto Schmidt/AFP/Getty Images; (c) IOC/Olympic Museum Collections; (bl) Jamie Squire/Getty Images; (tr) Bettmann/Corbis; (br) Shaun Best/Reuters/Corbis; 12 (t) IOC Olympic Museum/ Allsport/Getty Images; (b) Underwood & Underwood/Corbis; 12-13 Underwood & Underwood/Corbis; 14 (t) Swim Ink/Corbis; (b) Time Life Pictures/Getty Images; 15 S&G/Empics/Alpha; 16 Staff/AFP/Getty Images; 17 (both) Topical Press Agency/Getty Images; 18 (both) Bettmann/Corbis; 20 (t) Collection of the Author; (b) Staff/AFP/Getty Images; 20-21 Staff/AFP/Getty Images; 22 Hulton Archive/Getty Images; 23 Ernst Haas/Getty Images; 24-25 Andrew Winning/Reuters/Corbis; 26 George Silk/Time Life Pictures/Getty Images; 27 Wally McNamee/Corbis; 28 (t) IOC Olympic Museum/ Allsport/Getty Images; (b) Bettmann/Corbis; 28-29 Bettmann/Corbis; 30 AP/Wide World Photos; 31 New York Times Co./Getty Images; 32 Bettmann/Corbis; 33 Bettmann/ Corbis; 34 (t) AP/Wide World Photos; (b) Stan Wayman/Time Life Pictures/Getty Images; 35 IOC Olympic Museum/Allsport/Getty Images; 36-37 Bettmann/Corbis; 38 Steve Powell/Getty Images; 39 (t) AP/Wide World Photos; (b) Michael Probst/Reuters/Corbis; 40 (t) Clive Brunskill/Getty Images; (b) Dominique Faget/AFP/Getty Images; 41 Mike Powell/Allsport/Getty Images; 42 (tl) AP/Wide World Photos/Elise Amendola; (lc) AP/Wide World Photos/Paul Sakuma; (bl) Clive Brunskill/ Allsport/Getty Images; (tr) Kazuhiro Nogi/AFP/Getty Images; (br) FPG/Getty Images; 43 (tl) Hulton-Deutsch Collection/Corbis; (bl) Adrian Dennis/AFP/Getty Images; (c) IOC/Olympic Museum Collections; (tr) AP/Wide World Photos/Laura Rauch; (br) Central Press/Getty Images; 44 (t) IOC/Olympic Museum Collections; (b) Paul Harvath/Corbis Sygma; 44-45 Paul Harvath/Corbis Sygma; 46 Jerry Lampen/Reuters/Corbis; 47 (t) Clive Brunskill/Allsport/Getty Images; (b) Blake Sell/Reuters/Corbis; 48 Caron/Corbis Sygma; 49 Staff/AFP/Getty Images; 50 (t) Bettmann/Corbis; (b) Staff/AFP/Getty Images; 53 (t) Steven Sutton/Duomo/Corbis; (b) Paul Sutton/Duomo/Corbis; 54-55 Hulton Archive/Getty Images; 56 Clive Brunskill/Getty Images; 57 AP/Wide World Photos/Laurent Rebours; 58 (t) Dennis Nazari/Utah Snowboard Museum; (b) Adrian Dennis/AFP/Getty Images; 58-59 Adrian Dennis/AFP/Getty Images; 60 AP/Wide World Photos/Laura Rauch; 61 Jeff J. Mitchell/Reuters/Corbis; 62-63 Clive Mason/Getty Images; 64 Ezra Shaw/Getty Images; 65 Don Emmert/AFP/Getty Images; 66 AP/Wide World Photos/Douglas C. Pizac; 67 Matthew Stockman/ Allsport/Getty Images; 68 (tl) AP/Wide World Photos/David J. Phillip; (lc) George Frey/AFP/Getty Images; (bl) Leonhard Foeger/Reuters/Corbis; (tr) Bettmann/Corbis; (br) Adrian Dennis/AFP/Getty Images; 69 (tl) Jerry Lampen/Reuters/Corbis; (bl) Paul Sutton/Duomo/Corbis; (tr) Jeff J. Mitchell/Reuters/Corbis; (br) Gary M. Prior/Getty Images; 73 (t) AP/Wide World Photos/Amy Sancetta; (b) Bettmann/Corbis; 74 S&G/Empics/Alpha; 75 (both) IOC Olympic Museum/Allsport/Getty Images; 76 (t) IOC Olympic Museum/Allsport/Getty Images; (b) Bettmann/Corbis; 77 (t) Swim Ink 2, LLC/Corbis; (b) Collection of the Author; 78 IOC Olympic Museum/Allsport/ Getty Images; 79 (t) IOC Olympic Museum/Allsport/Getty Images; (b) Bettmann/Corbis; 80 (t) Bettmann/Corbis; (b) IOC Olympic Museum/Allsport/ Getty Images; 81 (t) IOC Olympic Museum/Allsport/Getty Images; (b) Staff/AFP/Getty Images; 82 (t) IOC Olympic Museum/Allsport/ Getty Images; (b) UN DA-SIN/AFP/Getty Images; 83 (br) AP/Wide World Photos/Michel Lipchitz; 84 (t) Collection of the Author; (b) IOC Olympic Museum/Allsport/ Getty Images; 85 (t) IOC Olympic Museum/ Allsport/Getty Images; (b) AP/Wide World Photos/Vincenzo Giaco; 86 (t) IOC Olympic Museum/Allsport/ Getty Images; (b) George Gobet/AFP/Getty Images; 87 (t) IOC Olympic Museum/Allsport/Getty Images; (b) Collection of the Author; 88 Junji Kurokawa/AFP/Getty Images; 89 (t) Jiji Press/AFP/Getty Images; (b) AP/Wide World Photos/Paul Chiasson; 90 (t) Sean Gallup/Getty Images; (b) Handout/Reuters/Corbis; 91 John Gichigi/Getty Images.

One of the world's largest nonprofit scientific and educational organizations, the National Geographic Society was founded in 1888 "for the increase and diffusion of geographic knowledge." Fulfilling this mission, the Society educates and inspires millions every day through its magazines, books, television programs, videos, maps and atlases, research grants, the National Geographic Bee, teacher workshops, and innovative classroom materials. The Society is supported through membership dues, charitable gifts, and income from the sale of its educational products. This support is vital to National Geographic's mission to increase global understanding and promote conservation of our planet through exploration, research, and education.

For more information, please call 1-800-NGS-LINE (647-5463) or write to the following address:

National Geographic Society
1145 17th Street, N.W.
Washington, D.C. 20036-4688 U.S.A.

Visit the Society's Web site:
www.nationalgeographic.com

PUBLISHED BY THE NATIONAL GEOGRAPHIC SOCIETY

John M. Fahey, Jr., *President and Chief Executive Officer*

Gilbert M. Grosvenor, *Chairman of the Board*

Nina D. Hoffman, *Executive Vice President, President of Books and Education*

Ericka Markman, *Senior Vice President, President of Children's Books and Education*

Stephen Mico, *Publisher, Vice President of Children's Books and Education*

STAFF FOR THIS BOOK

Nancy Laties Feresten, *Vice President, Editor-in-Chief of Children's Books*

Bea Jackson, *Design Director, Children's Books and Education*

Margaret Sidlosky, *Illustrations Director, Children's Books and Education*

Jennifer Emmett, *Project Editor*

Marty Ittner, *Designer*

Jean Cantu, *Illustrations Coordinator*

Carl Mehler, *Director of Maps*

Priyanka Lamichhane, *Editorial Assistant*

R. Gary Colbert, *Production Director*

Lewis R. Bassford, *Production Manager*

Vincent P. Ryan, *Manufacturing Manager*